Does God Care for Oxen?

Does God Care for Oxen?

Recovering the Biblical Doctrine of Stewardship

Ruben Alvarado

WordBridge
PUBLISHING
εν αρχη ην ο λογος
AALTEN, THE NETHERLANDS

WORDBRIDGE PUBLISHING
Aalten, the Netherlands
www.wordbridge.net
info@wordbridge.net

ISBN 978–90–76660–71–4

COVER ILLUSTRATION: "The Entry of the Animals into Noah's Ark" by Jan Brueghel the Elder (1613). The inside cover illustration is "The 12 Tribes in Military Order with the Levites roundabout the Tabernacle," taken from Petrus Cunaeus, *De Republyk der Hebreen* (Amsterdam: Andries van Damme, 1704), vol. 2, facing p. 506. Both representations are in the public domain.

expanded

TABLE OF CONTENTS

DEDICATION

To E. Calvin Beisner, one of the happy few Christian academics who continue to stand in the gap for Scriptural truth.

INTRODUCTION

There are many verses in the Bible which treat of the natural creation. Many of them pass in review whenever one consults any of the myriad writings put forward by Christian environmentalists. But there is one passage which is ignored entirely. It is the passage which inspired the title of this book.

In his first letter to the church in Corinth, Paul finds himself defending his ministry in the face of accusations that he was exploiting the church for material gain. Even if he were receiving material benefit from the church – and he makes clear that he had not been – it would not be wrong for him to do so. "Who goes to warfare any time at his own expense? who plants a vineyard, and eats not of the fruit thereof? or who feeds a flock, and eats not of the milk of the flock?" (1 Corinthians 9: 7, King James 2000 version, and so throughout this section). Hence, it was his perfect right to do so, even though he chose not to make use of that right. "Even so has the Lord ordained that they who preach the gospel should live of the gospel. But I have used none of these things" (vv. 14–15).

Such a right, Paul says, is not based in human reasoning but is grounded in the Torah, the Old Testament law. "Say I these things as a man? or says not the law the same also?" (v. 8). And which law is it that he then adduces? One regulating the care of animals! "For it is written in the law of Moses, You shall not muzzle the mouth of the ox that treads out the grain." (v. 9). What does that have to do with material provision for preachers of the gospel? *Everything.* To wit: "Does God care for oxen? Or says he it altogether for our sakes? For our sakes, no doubt, this is written: that he that plows should plow in hope; and that he that threshes in hope should be partaker of his hope." (vv. 9–10). God is speaking *altogether* [pantós] for our sake. That means entirely, completely. In other words, God does not care so much about animals as He cares about us. The Torah, even in its provisions regulating how animals are to be cared for, is for the benefit of human beings.

"This is a hard saying; who can hear it?" (John 6: 60). It is no wonder that this verse lies fallow, as it were, among the many that are diligently cultivated in Christian environmentalist literature. But it surely is a sign that something is not quite right.

Might this reticence be explained by the fear that such a verse could be twisted into an apology for the unfettered exploitation of the natural world? One school of thought teaches precisely such an outcome. In its view, Christianity is to blame for the "ecologic crisis," to use Lynn White's term.

Yes, even before the publication of White's famous article[1] – in fact, ever since the publication of Aldo Leopold's *A Sand County Almanac* in 1949 – it been fashionable to blame Christianity for the pressure put on nature by human civilization.

Now the critique of civilization itself goes back far beyond 1949; in 1864, George Perkins Marsh's *Man and Nature* had already highlighted the degradations of the natural habitat suffered through the impact of human populations on countries surrounding the Mediterranean, and indeed Tertullian (155–230 A. D.) had already complained of them. What was new was that Christianity should get the blame.

And we can see the agenda behind this blame game. Humanism had previously championed the triumph of man over nature, especially since the Industrial Revolution. The control of the natural environment, the exercise of exuberant powers over previously malignant forces of nature were celebrated in paeans to autonomous man. Prometheus had outgrown the need for the supernatural for survival and had kicked away the crutch provided by religion in the face of those inscrutable forces. But then forces of another sort were unleashed, and now they seemed out of control. "Modern science, and the huge technological enterprises which it produces, represent the full flowering of man's understanding of nature. Scientific knowledge is our best guide to controlling natural forces. In this it has been magnificently successful; it is this success which has given us the marvels of modern electricity, and the tremendous power of nuclear bombs.... Are we really in control of the vast new powers that science has given us, or is there a danger that science is getting out of hand?"[2] Man had become, in Commoner's words, a "Sorcerer's Apprentice." A scapegoat had to be found, now that he had revealed himself to be a poor

---

[1] "The Historic Roots of Our Ecologic Crisis."
[2] Commoner, *Science and Survival,* pp. 7–8.

master of the universe; and that scapegoat – not for the first time – was Christianity. It was Christianity which was to blame for progress, for industrialization, for the loss of contact with the natural environment.

Thus guilted into feeling responsible for the situation, church leaders went to work developing a response to the prickling accusation, one which pursues common ground with the secular environmental movement. To this end, they dusted off an accoutrement of ecclesiastical bustle, the doctrine of stewardship,[3] and they fashioned it into an ideology whereby the Scriptural injunctions toward right living as an outworking of salvation granted in Christ could be applied to the environmental crisis. Hereby humanity is invoked as both problem and solution, using the church's framework of sin and grace, lost and saved. Lost humanity is then humanity which exploits and domineers the natural creation, and saved humanity is humanity which nurtures and seeks the well-being of the natural creation. It is all a matter of regaining a lost Eden through the efforts of men and women of good will everywhere.

A wide range of Scripture is applied to bolster this framework. The question is whether this is done responsibly. Does Scripture really advocate such an expansive doctrine? How indeed does nature function within the Scriptural framework? In view of the fact that a certain ideology of stewardship has been elevated to the status of Christian duty, indeed to the status of love of neighbor[4] (of which there is no greater com-

---

[3] "We are unexpectedly witnessing in secular society the rebirth of a biblical and 'church' word that twenty years ago many thought had had its day. That word is 'stewardship.' A generation or two ago its use was widespread in Christian circles, especially among Protestants. Although the term has a relatively limited usage in the New Testament, during the 1940s, '50s, and '60s it enjoyed a wide currency among Christians in discussions of God's goodness, particularly with respect to money and other material resources. Then it went out of style, and only a few fought a rearguard action in parishes or denominations here and there to keep it in use." Reumann, *Stewardship and the Economy of God*, p. 1.

[4] "Who, finally, is my *neighbor*...? ... He is man and he is angel and he is animal and inorganic being, all that participates in being." Niebuhr, *The Purpose of the Church*, p. 38.

mandment – Mark 12: 31), and is being thrust upon believers whether they like it or not, an answer to that question is of the utmost importance. That is what this book aims to provide.

THE RISE OF THE ENVIRONMENTAL MOVEMENT

The environmental movement did not always enjoy the towering influence it does today. It really came into its own in the 1960s, with the publication of Rachel Carson's book *Silent Spring*. A retiring biologist who passed away from cancer not long after *Silent Spring's* publication, Carson was an unlikely champion of a popular movement. But *Silent Spring* became a talisman which inspired the banning of the pesticide DDT and otherwise kicked off a movement that, combined with nascent anti-industrialism and pacifism, constituted a turning point in the public mind. Population control was a consistent fellow-traveler in the recurring doomsday scenarios that from then on littered the media landscape. The now-familiar refrains of impending catastrophe through human interference in nature's benign economy began their march to familiarity and hegemony.

Charles Reich's bestseller *The Greening of America* (1970) gave voice to the movement.

> There is a revolution coming, not... like revolutions of the past. It will originate with the individual and with culture, and it will change the political structure only as its final act. It will not require violence to succeed, and it cannot be successfully resisted by violence. It is now spreading with amazing rapidity, and already our laws, institutions and social structure are changing in consequence. It promises a higher reason, a more human community, and a new and liberated individual. Its ultimate creation will be a new and enduring wholeness and beauty—a renewed relationship of man to himself, to other men, to society, to nature, and to the land.[5]

The younger generation – today we know them as the Boomers[6] – led

---

[5] Reich, *The Greening of America,* pp. 13–14.
[6] Let no one say that the Boomers include anyone born between 1945 and 1965, as is the practice today. Boomers originally were known as those born in the *im-*

the way:

> This is the revolution of the new generation. Their protest and rebellion, their culture, clothes, music, drugs, ways of thought, and liberated life-style are not a passing fad or a form of dissent and refusal, nor are they in any sense irrational. The whole emerging pattern, from ideals to campus demonstrations to beads and bell bottoms to the Woodstock Festival, makes sense and is part of a consistent philosophy. It is both necessary and inevitable, and in time it will include not only youth, but all people in America.[7]

So for Reich, what this meant was the triumph of humanity, and of nature, over technology. "Beyond the industrial era lies a new age of man. The essence of that age must be the end of the subjugation of man, the end of his subordination to the machine, and the beginning of the subjugation of the machine—the use of technology to create a still higher level of life, but one based upon values beyond the machine."[8]

As a result, instead of rejecting the productive capacity of modern society, Reich celebrated it as the platform upon which the new revolutionary way of life could be built. "Since machines can produce enough food and shelter for all, why should not man end the antagonism derived from scarcity and base his society on love for his fellow man? If machines can take care of our material wants, why should not man develop the aesthetic and spiritual side of his nature? Prophets and philosophers have proposed these ways of life before, but only today's technology has made them possible."[9]

But this was not nearly enough for Barry Commoner. His book *The*

---

mediate wake of the Second World War, during the so-called "baby boom." They were characterized by a certain sense of entitlement produced by the coddling they received from their parents, the so-called "Greatest Generation." Those of us born in their shadow, thus in the late 1950s/early 1960s, tended to look upon them with trepidation, as the people responsible for casting a shadow over our childhoods in their zeal to upset settled certainties and established authorities.

[7] Reich, *The Greening of America,* p. 14.
[8] Reich, *The Greening of America,* p. 310.
[9] Reich, *The Greening of America,* p. 308.

Closing Circle, published in 1971, upped the ante.

"Earth Day" held in 1970 opened many eyes. "The environment has just been rediscovered by the people who live in it," he wrote. "In the United States the event was celebrated in April 1970, during Earth Week. It was a sudden, noisy awakening. School children cleaned up rubbish; college students organized huge demonstrations; determined citizens recaptured the streets from the automobile, at least for a day. Everyone seemed to be aroused to the environmental danger and eager to do something about it."[10]

All of a sudden, everyone was an environmentalist, but likewise everyone had an opinion on the matter, not all of which were helpful. "It seemed to me that the confusion of Earth Week was a sign that the situation was so complex and ambiguous that people could read into it whatever conclusion their own beliefs—about human nature, economics, and politics—suggested. Like a Rorschach ink blot, Earth Week mirrored personal convictions more than objective knowledge."[11]

So Commoner took it upon himself to clarify the matter: *pace* Reich, it was precisely technology, the machine and the production process built upon it, that was the problem.

> The environmental crisis is somber evidence of an insidious fraud hidden in the vaunted productivity and wealth of modern, technology-based society. This wealth has been gained by rapid short-term exploitation of the environmental system, but it has blindly accumulated a debt to nature (in the form of environmental destruction in developed countries and of population pressure in developing ones)—a debt so large and so pervasive that in the next generation it may, if unpaid, wipe out most of the wealth it has gained us.[12]

It is production – machine production, industrial production – that is the problem. What once was celebrated for lifting man above the vicis-

---

[10] Commoner, *The Closing Circle,* p. 5.
[11] Commoner, *The Closing Circle,* p. 10.
[12] Commoner, *The Closing Circle,* p. 295.

situdes of nature was now excoriated for having done precisely that. Machines enabled mankind to outstrip nature's ability to provide, resulting in the population explosion. Mankind must learn to live within the boundaries set by nature.

And this ecological crisis is but a facet of the all-embracing problem-set facing civilization. For the environmental crisis is intertwined with other, familiar problems, and therefore has to be solved together with these other problems – and in the familiar way.

> To resolve the environmental crisis, we shall need to forego, at last, the luxury of tolerating poverty, racial discrimination, and war. In our unwitting march toward ecological suicide we have run out of options. Now that the bill for the environmental debt has been presented, our options have become reduced to two: either the rational, social organization of the use and distribution of the earth's resources, or a new barbarism.[13]

All roads lead to Rome, or at least to the kind of centralized distributional power that governmentalists have yearned for since time immemorial. Let us see how the church responded to this challenge.

---

[13] Commoner, *The Closing Circle*, p. 296.

THE RISE OF THE CHRISTIAN ENVIRONMENTAL MOVEMENT

> In recent times the gap between traditional moral principles and the re-
> alities of modern life has become so large as to precipitate, beginning in
> the Catholic church, and less spectacularly in other religious denomina-
> tions, urgent demands for renewal—for the development of statements
> of moral purpose which are directly relevant to the modern world. But
> in the modern world the substance of moral issues cannot be perceived
> in terms of the casting of stones or the theft of a neighbor's ox.[14]

Under the influence of this kind of goading, the church came around.
Along with the other headliners important to Boomers, environmentalism came to be embraced as a challenge not only to the world but to believers. Solidarity became the watchword, this earth being a possession
shared by all men and women of good will; and Christians could appeal
to the doctrine of creation to solidify that call to protect "the environment," to save "the planet." The Bible, Christians argued, established
man's vocation as steward of the environment, God's representative on
Earth to care for His good creation.

In fact (and perhaps to Commoner's surprise), the Bible seemed to
provide an arsenal of proof texts to demonstrate the validity of the environmentalist program. It spoke of God creating this planet and creating
it *good*. And of His then planting a garden in Eden, a place for His own
presence in the midst of this good earth. God created man and woman,
calling the man "Adam," Hebrew for "of the earth," by which we are given
to understand that man is intimately interwoven into the natural creation. And God put Adam into the garden of Eden and commanded him,
so the common translations go, to "cultivate it and to keep it" as Genesis
2: 15 puts it. The implications, it would seem, are clear:

> Cultivating certainly implies some change, growth and development. But
> it is growth and change of a positive, constructive nature, as when we

---

[14] Commoner, *Science and Survival,* p. 130.

speak of "cultivating" a friendship. It means to assist something to achieve its own natural and highest tendencies. The Hebrew understanding of this concept was stronger. The word translated "cultivate" (*'ābad*) comes from the Hebrew word meaning "to serve" or, more literally, "to be a slave to." In an agrarian society, it was natural to think of cultivation in this way. How else would one "serve" the ground?

And we all know what "keeping" means. It means to preserve, protect and maintain. The fact that both are here used to describe Adam's care of the same object, Eden, can only mean that neither God nor Adam viewed them as conflicting goals. To subdue Eden apparently meant to retain the goodness and beauty which God gave it, while actively serving Eden through managing (cultivating) it to better enhance and manifest the qualities hidden within it. The Hebrew word *šāmar*, translated as "keep" in English, is the same word used in the familiar benediction of Numbers 6: 22–26. Moses is instructed to tell Aaron and his sons to bless the Israelites with these words, "The Lord bless you and keep [*šāmar*] you; the Lord make his face shine upon you and be gracious to you; the Lord turn his face toward you and give you peace." Clearly humankind is instructed to "keep" the garden as the Lord "keeps" us.[15]

This, then, was man's mission: to dress and keep this precious garden of Eden, this good Earth, "this vast, dynamic, beautiful, but suffering planet," for "heaven and earth are the Lord's, the product of the Creator's ongoing love—a love which calls us, through creation and through Christ, back to our original task in creation, which is to be gardeners of the earth, stewards of what God has entrusted to us."[16]

But this original trust was not kept. Adam's fall from innocence into sinfulness resulted in God's cursing the ground because of him, a curse which has since manifested itself in his abuse of the natural creation which was given in trust to him. In this manner the creation has been "subjected to futility"; it is in "slavery to corruption"; it "groans and suffers the pains of childbirth until now," waiting to enter into "the freedom

---

[15] Van Dyke et al., *Redeeming Creation*, p. 96.
[16] Wilkinson, *Earthkeeping in the Nineties*, p. x.

of the glory of the children of God" (Romans 8: 20–22).[17]

Various passages, it is averred, give voice to this sad state of affairs. Isaiah highlights man's abuse of nature in passages like these: "The earth mourns and withers, the world fades and withers, the exalted of the people of the earth fade away. The earth is also polluted by its inhabitants, for they transgressed laws, violated statutes, broke the everlasting covenant. Therefore, a curse devours the earth, and those who live in it are held guilty. Therefore, the inhabitants of the earth are burned, and few men are left" (24: 4–6).

The laws transgressed, the statutes violated, are those which were given by Moses to Israel. Among the various stipulations contained in this Torah which regulate the treatment of the natural creation, are the Sabbath laws. The land is to be given its Sabbath rests:

Six years you shall sow your field, and six years you shall prune your vineyard and gather in its crop, but during the seventh year the land shall have a sabbath rest, a sabbath to the LORD; you shall not sow your field nor prune your vineyard. Your harvest's aftergrowth you shall not reap, and your grapes of untrimmed vines you shall not gather; the land shall have a sabbatical year. And all of you shall have the sabbath products of the land for food; yourself, and your male and female slaves, and your hired man and your foreign resident, those who live as aliens with you. Even your cattle and the animals that are in your land shall have all its crops to eat (Leviticus 25: 3–7).

Here express provision is made not only for the land but also for servants, hirelings, foreigners, livestock, and wild animals – "all its growth may serve as food" for them.

But the land was not given its Sabbath rest. This was the reason why Israel was punished and carried away into exile in Babylon. Seventy years of exile allowed the land to recover from centuries of exploitation. "So the land enjoyed its Sabbath rest all the days of the desolation, until sev-

---

[17] Unless otherwise noted, quotations from the Bible are from the New American Standard Bible, 1977 edition.

enty years were completed, in fulfillment of the word of the Lord through Jeremiah" (2 Chronicles 36: 21, Berean Study Bible [BSB]). As Van Dyke et al. put it, "The tragedy of exile came upon Israel for many reasons, but it is noteworthy that the only reason given in this passage was for Israel's abuse of the land."[18]

And as Israel was punished in the Babylonian captivity, so will civilization be punished in the End Time for its crimes against the natural world. In the Book of Revelation, the apostle John speaks of that time as harboring judgment, to "destroy those who destroy the earth" (11: 18). For environmental destruction? Indeed: "The punishment is extreme because God considers such destruction an extreme sin."[19]

The message is clear: God is deeply concerned with nature and will punish man's abuse of it.

[18] Van Dyke et al., *Redeeming Creation*, p. 79.
[19] Van Dyke et al., *Redeeming Creation*, p. 125.

WHAT THE BIBLE ACTUALLY SAYS ABOUT THE NATURAL CREATION

The question, though, is whether this line of interpretation accurately reflects what Scripture has to say on the subject.

Beginning with the beginning: the good creation. What does it mean when God calls His creation "good," even "very good"? The received understanding of this is "perfect" – but is that what is here being said?

Old Testament scholar John Walton argues that this is not the case.

> Interpreters have often concluded that in order for that world to be "good," there must have been no pain, no suffering, no death and no predation; everything was pristine and perfect.... In this way of thinking, one can infer what "good" means by drawing a contrast with the state of sin after the fall. The conclusion is that anything that is negative in our experience did not exist in that primeval world. As popular as this view is, in reality the word never carries this sense of unadulterated, pristine perfection.[20]

In fact, the Hebrew word for "good" carries a good many other meanings than "perfect," and these can only be discerned by referring to the context in which it occurs. In this case, the context is function, just as function is the context for Gen. 2: 18, "it is not good for the man to be alone." In this case, then, "good" means the establishment of "a functional, ordered system."[21] This echoes the judgment of Claus Westermann: "In any case 'good' is not to be understood as indicating some fixed quality; the meaning is rather functional: 'good for....' The world which God created and devised as good is the world in which history can begin and reach its goal and so fulfill the purpose of creation."[22] Dumbrell offers a similar conclusion: "What this must mean is that creation corresponds to the purposes for which it was destined, i.e., it conformed to God's pur-

---

[20] *The Lost World of Adam and Eve*, p. 53.

[21] *The Lost World of Adam and Eve*, p. 56.

[22] *Genesis 1–11*, p. 166.

poses."[23]

Granted, this is not the usual interpretation of the text, which indeed views God's declaration of the goodness of what He created as indicating pristineness, perfection. Rather, it simply indicates goodness with regard to the purpose for which it was created, which might very well include *un*pristineness and *im*perfection.

Just so, for in fact there are good biblical grounds to view the creation precisely as harboring unpristineness and imperfection.

For one thing, why was there a Garden of Eden? This garden is not a mere part of the rest of the creation. It is not just another piece of land. In fact it is set apart and protected from the rest of the creation. "The Hebrew word *gan* 'garden' refers to a fenced-off enclosure (Hb. *ganan* 'cover', 'protect', 'enclose') protected by a wall or hedge. Walls as surrounding royal gardens are specifically mentioned in the Old Testament (2 Kgs 25:4; Neh. 3:15; Jer. 39:4; 52:7). The Garden of Eden is thus a special place that is spatially separated from an outside world presumably very much like our own present world."[24]

Why this separation? If the earth is pristine and perfect, why put an isolated Garden of Eden in its midst? Could it be that the earth was *not* created pristine and perfect? The apostle Paul has something to say which, although hitherto overlooked, sheds needed light on the matter.

In 1 Corinthians 15, Paul goes into detail about the difference between the original, supposedly "pristine" Adam – Adam before his fall into sin – and the resurrected Christ. He does so to draw a contrast between what he calls the "natural" body and the "spiritual" body, the "natural" body being the unfallen Adam and the "spiritual" body being the resurrected Christ. Paul compares this natural body to a seed that is sown; and he avers that it is "sown a perishable body... sown in dishonor... sown in weakness..." (vv. 42, 43). Perishable, dishonorable, weak – this does not sound like it answers to the pristine and perfect condition claimed by the traditional interpretation.

But Paul goes further.

So also it is written, "The first man, Adam, became a living soul." The last

---

[23] *The End of the Beginning*, p. 177.

[24] Dumbrell, *Covenant and Creation*, p. 57.

Adam became a life-giving spirit. However, the spiritual is not first, but the natural; then the spiritual. The first man is from the earth, earthy; the second man is from heaven. As is the earthy, so also are those who are earthy; and as is the heavenly, so also are those who are heavenly (vv. 45–48).

Paul here quotes Genesis 2: 7, which states that God created Adam from the ground and breathed the breath of life into him, whereby Adam became a living soul. As such, he is of the earth, earthy. Earlier we noted that this characteristic of the original Adam is cited to show his solidarity with the created, natural world. Indeed. "As is the earthy, so also are those who are earthy." But is this a "good" thing? What does Paul then say about it? "Now I say this, brethren, that flesh and blood cannot inherit the kingdom of God; nor does the perishable inherit the imperishable" (v. 50). Precisely the opposite of what the proponents of solidarity with the natural world would have us believe. In fact, being earthy – as the opposite of being heavenly (vv. 47–49) – *stands in the way* of our inheriting the kingdom of God. As we are, we cannot enter into that kingdom; but neither could Adam, *even before he fell.* God created Adam, and the natural world with him, earthy, entailing perishability, dishonor, and weakness.

Earthiness is contrasted with spiritualness in other verses as well. There is John 3: 31: "He who comes from above is above all, he who is of the earth is from the earth and speaks of the earth. He who comes from heaven is above all." So earthiness is nothing to be proud of, but rather an acknowledgment of spiritual blindness. And Philippians 3: 19: "... whose end is destruction, whose god is their appetite, and whose glory is in their shame, who set their minds on earthly things." Solidarity with the earth indeed. And James 3: 15: "This wisdom is not that which comes down from above, but is earthly, natural, demonic." Far from pure and pristine, that which is earthly and natural (the same word which is used by Paul, quoting Gen. 2: 7, where it is written that God created Adam a living *soul)* is put on a line with... the demonic? Yes indeed.

What is it about earthiness that is so opposed to spiritualness? 1 Cor. 15: 50 enlightens us further. It tells us that the perishable cannot inherit the imperishable. Now the Greek word for "perishable" or "what is per-

ishable" is *phthora,* which means corruption. What is earthy, then, is perishable, corruptible. Its earthiness needs to be transformed. That is what
Christ accomplished in His death and resurrection. For in the resurrection of His body He works the resurrection of Adam's body as well.

This extends to all of creation. "For it was the Father's good pleasure
for all the fulness to dwell in Him, and through Him to reconcile all
things to Himself, having made peace through the blood of His cross;
through Him, I say, whether things on earth or things in heaven" (Colos-
sians 1: 19–20). And when we realize this, we also have the key to understanding the supposed proof text of man's abuse of the natural world, Romans 8: 19–23. There it says that the creation was "subjected to futility,
not of its own will, but because of Him who subjected it" (v. 20). As such,
this subjection comes through an act of God not man. And in what con-
sists this subjection to futility? Paul elaborates further: it is a "slavery to
corruption" (v. 21) – *phthora,* the same word that Paul uses in 1 Corinthians 15 to describe Adam's condition as created.

This is key. For this corruption, by Paul's own admission in 1 Cor. 15,
is part of the original creation. Therefore, this passage in Romans 8 *cannot
refer to the fall,* neither as God's response to man's sin, nor as the condition
of the creation after the fall. Just as the passage in 1 Corinthians 15, this
passage in Romans 8 refers to the condition of the creation *prior* to the
fall.

So what is it about which the creation "groans and suffers the pains of
childbirth"? Is it fallen man's abuse of the natural world, as our Christian
environmentalists would have it? Not at all! It is the condition of the natural world *by virtue of creation.* It is waiting to be released from its *earthiness!*

What are we being told here? That God *created* the natural world in
slavery to corruption, in subjection to futility? Precisely. But it was created good, even very good! Yes – but as we have seen, that does not mean
pristine, it means something else. It means being exactly suited to the purpose for which it is created. I need not explain that purpose in any detail
here, as I have set it forth elsewhere.[25] What it means is that the *original*
natural world is in slavery to corruption and in subjection to futility.[26]

---

[25] Chapter 8, "The Purpose of God in Creation," in *A Theology of Nature.*
[26] For a detailed outworking of this, see *A Theology of Nature.*

This means that the natural world was neither pristine nor perfect. It was created in a condition of corruption, death, and decay. From the start, it could not inherit the kingdom of God. It needed transformation. It was sown a natural body; it will be raised a spiritual body. And it is precisely this for which it "waits in eager expectation for the revelation of the sons of God" (v. 19). For the resurrection of man will bring with it the renewal of all creation. It is for this that it "groans and suffers the pains of child-birth"; it awaits, as we do, "our adoption as sons, the redemption of our bodies" (v. 23).

That Christians who follow the traditional interpretation will have a difficult time accepting this, stands to reason. It runs against the grain. As such, it is understandable that the theologians who contribute to the discussion about stewardship of the environment easily embrace the notion of a pristine world before Adam's fall. The traditional interpretation dovetails nicely with the idea of the natural world untouched by man as in tune with itself, in balance with itself, indeed the Garden of Eden writ large, whereby (fallen) man is cast as the interloper, the violator, the despoiler. But the real natural world is something quite different from the romanticized fluff that in this manner is presented to us, and natural scientists are aware of that. They know that nature truly is red in tooth and claw; it truly is in a constant state of flux, never in balance[27]; it has no standard of right and wrong, unless we accept Aldo Leopold's dictum: "A thing is right when it tends to preserve the integrity, stability, and beauty

------

[27] As the distinguished natural scientist Daniel Botkin has shown in great detail. See *Discordant Harmonies* and *25 Myths That Are Destroying the Environment*. For his part, Young attempts to have it both ways, arguing both for and against the idea of a balance of nature: "It is becoming increasingly obvious that the entire earth, including humanity, constitutes one large ecosystem, which will continue to support life as we know it only if the 'balance of nature' is maintained or kept within a certain range of tolerance.... One must not perceive this 'balance of nature' as a static, ideal state. Ecosystems are amazingly dynamic and resilient. The idea of a perfect state of equilibrium or balance of nature is somewhat of a myth." *Healing the Earth,* p. 53.

of the biotic community. It is wrong when it tends otherwise."[28] Which is a nice way of saying that death, decay, parasitism, saprophytism, and all the other unsavory aspects of nature are actually expressions of justice (who knew?). Theologians, we can understand; Christian natural scientists should know better than to bloviate about the pristine sanctity and the delicate balance of the natural world.[29]

---

[28] *A Sand County Almanac*, pp. 224–225.

[29] As they do profusely in the *Earthkeeping* books and in *Redeeming Creation*, among others.

GARDEN AND TEMPLE

With this preliminary understanding of Scripture we can now turn to address the passages said to advance the idea of Christian environmentalism and planetary stewardship.[30]

Genesis 1–2

Let us begin by looking at what is perhaps the keystone verse for understanding man's relationship to nature: "Then the Lord God took the man and placed him in the Garden of Eden to cultivate and keep it" (Genesis 2: 15). As we have seen, this verse is supposed to call us to stewardship of the natural world. It is understood to explain man's vocation as given by God: to engage in farming and gardening in such a way that the natural environment is maintained in beauty, health, and splendor – thus not exploited but nurtured. Man's vocation, then, is understood to be nature-centric stewardship, as if nature were the end (τέλος, goal) of creation. But a closer examination of the text yields a starkly different conclusion.

First, there is the circumstance already noted, that by establishing a garden in Eden, God set apart an area from the wider natural world. Dumbrell elaborates further: "This makes the garden a special place which is spatially separated from its outside world." Why this separation? Because it is "a world which needs to be brought under the dominion of the divine rule for which Eden is a model."[31] As Beale argues, "[Adam and Eve] were on the primeval hillock of hospitable Eden, outside of which lay the inhospitable land. They were to extend the smaller liveable area of the garden by transforming the outer chaotic region into a habitable territory."[32] And Beisner: "It would have made little sense to tell Adam to

---

[30] Beisner's discussion of environmentalists' use of Scripture should also be consulted: "The Use of Scripture by Evangelical Environmentalists," ch. 4 in *Where Garden Meets Wilderness*.

[31] *Covenant and Creation*, p. 57.

[32] *The Temple and the Church's Mission*, p. 81.

subdue and rule the Garden. It was already in perfect order, and succeed-ing Biblical imagery indicates that it was a type of both the sanctuary and the New Jerusalem—and through them of heaven itself. But the rest of the earth apparently lacked some of the fullness of the perfection of the Garden. It was Adam's task to transform all of the earth (to subdue and rule it) into a Garden while guarding the original Garden lest it lose some of its perfection and become like the unsubdued earth."[33] Thus there is a stark contrast between Eden and the outside world.

What the received interpretation does not sufficiently bring out is just how different, how special the Garden of Eden was vis-à-vis the surround-ing environment. The preconceived notion that all the earth was primeval and pure has dulled readers of Scripture to the hints Scripture provides which, taken together, yield an altogether different picture. For God dwells in Eden, not in the outside world. He creates Adam outside the Garden and puts him in it. He brings animals to Adam from outside the Garden for him to name. When Adam falls, He expels him from the Gar-den, guarding against his re-entry by installing angelic cherubim as sen-tries, bearing flaming swords.

The true condition becomes even clearer when one realizes that Israel's tabernacle and temple are modeled on the original Garden of Eden. This is one of most fruitful results of recent biblical theology.[34] As models of the Garden of Eden, Israel's tabernacle and later temple incorporated holy-mountain imagery, replicated lush foliage, were festooned with gold and precious gems, and were represented as being the source of rivers of

---

[33] *Where Garden Meets Wilderness*, p. 13.

[34] Two sterling examples of which are Beale, *The Temple and the Church's Mis-sion*, and Morales, *Who Shall Ascend the Mountain of the Lord?* In Wenham's words, "The garden of Eden is not viewed by the author of Genesis simply as a piece of Mesopotamian farmland, but as an archetypal sanctuary, that is a place where God dwells and where man should worship him. Many of the features of the garden may also be found in later sanctuaries particularly the tabernacle or Jerusalem temple. These parallels suggest that the garden itself is understood as a sort of sanctuary." "Sanctuary Symbolism in the Garden of Eden Story," p. 19. In this article Wenham catalogs a whole range of likenesses between the Garden of Eden and the tabernacle/temple.

life. The menorah symbolized the Tree of Life.[35] The entrance to the tabernacle/temple was on the east, just as the cherubim were stationed at the east end of the Garden. Two of these same cherubim guarded the inner sanctuary of Solomon's temple (1 Kings 6: 23–28) and two others guarded the Ark of the Covenant.[36]

The tabernacle/temple harbored the presence of God while setting that presence off from the surrounding environs – this, not to protect God from the environment, but to protect the earthy, perishable environment from God, who is a consuming fire (Hebrews 12: 29; cf. Exodus 3: 2). Hence, the Garden of Eden was the first temple; or, to reverse the image, the subsequent tabernacle and temple were knockoffs of the Garden.

Given this understanding, we can comprehend the twofold vocation of man as established by God in Genesis 1 and 2. These two, while complementary, have different subject matters.

On the one hand, man is charged to be fruitful and multiply and fill the earth; he is charged to subdue it; he is charged to rule over the animals in it, "every living thing that moves on the earth" (v. 28). This is the so-called dominion or cultural mandate (of which more below).

On the other, man is charged to serve and guard the Garden. The two verbs here when taken together refer to temple service,[37] as is fitting for

---

[35] Wenham, "Sanctuary Symbolism in the Garden of Eden Story," p. 21.

[36] The description of Solomon's temple in 1 Kings 6 is especially redolent of Edenic themes.

[37] "The two Hebrew words for 'cultivate and keep' are usually translated 'serve and guard [or keep]' elsewhere in the Old Testament. It is true that the Hebrew word usually translated 'cultivate' can refer to an agricultural task when used by itself (e.g., 2:5; 3:23). When, however, these two words (verbal ['*ābad* and *šāmar*] and nominal forms) occur together in the Old Testament (within an approximately 15-word range), they refer either to Israelites 'serving' God and 'guarding [keeping]' God's word (approximately 10 times) or to priests who 'keep' the 'service' (or 'charge') of the tabernacle (see Num. 3:7–8; 8:25–26; 18:5–6; 1 Chr. 23:32; Ezek. 44:14)." Beale, *The Temple and the Church's Mission*, pp. 66–67. Cf. also Walton, *The Lost World of Adam and Eve*, pp. 104ff.; Wenham, "Sanctuary Symbolism in the Garden of Eden Story," p. 21.

the abode of God; they do not refer to gardening or farm work, *nor to any service rendered to nature at all*. This means that the received understanding of Gen. 2: 15 is entirely misguided and misleading. The work of priests is what is commanded here, in service to God, not nature. It was Adam's charge to serve in and preserve the Garden-Temple; failing in that, he was expelled from the Garden and had his place as guardian taken by the cherubim. For the charge given to Adam in Gen. 2: 15, "to guard" the Garden, is what the cherubim exercise *against* him in Gen. 3: 24.

So then: Adam was not expelled from the Garden for failing to implement best land-use practices. He was expelled for failing to guard the Garden from the Evil One and for disobeying God's injunction not to eat the fruit of the tree of the knowledge of good and evil.

The dominion mandate must be seen in the light of this temple service. Dominion is to be pursued in extension of that service. The two go together. As Beisner points out:

> God didn't tell man to protect the wilderness against the encroaching garden. He told man to protect the garden against the encroaching wilderness. God told Adam to protect the Garden; He did not tell Adam to protect all the rest of the earth. Rather, He told Adam to subdue and rule the rest of the earth. Indeed, we may infer from this and the general garden-versus-wilderness theme of Scripture that an implicit part of the cultural mandate was the gradual transformation of the rest of the earth into the garden.[38]

We can get an idea of this by envisioning the nation Israel as gathered roundabout the tabernacle, from which it proceeded to conquer the land of Canaan. This is what Genesis 1–2 has in mind. Only it was originally to be pursued into all the world; but when Adam and Eve fell, their vocation suffered a mortal blow that would take generations, centuries, millennia, to re-establish, through the covenantal history of Noah, Abraham, Moses, David, and finally Christ's salvific work for, in, and through the church.

The tabernacle and temple having had an Edenic character, they also had an Edenic effect. Through the temple service and in obedience to

---

[38] Beisner, *Where Garden Meets Wilderness,* p. 127.

God's law, by which room was once again made for God Himself to tabernacle with man, the curse on man's use of the natural world as put forward in Gen. 3: 17 was turned to blessing. Just this is what happened when the tabernacle was erected in Israel and God returned to dwell among His people, as described in Exodus ch. 40.

> For the first time since the primeval flood – since the expulsion from the garden of YHWH – God, through the tabernacle, will dwell amidst humanity. The maker of heaven and earth, who had once walked among humanity in the mists of the olden days before the flood, returns once more – *now* – in history, through a covenant relationship with Israel mediated by Moses. When the glory of YHWH descends upon the tabernacle, therefore, a historic cataclysmic event takes place: the God of heaven in all his thunderous majesty has arrived – the Advent of YHWH – to dwell with his people *on earth:* Eden regained.[39]

The covenantal and liturgical arrangement reverses the effects of the fall. The restored presence of God brings earthly blessing, and man is once again enabled to pursue his original mandate to be fruitful, multiply, fill the earth and subdue it.

Leviticus 26

Chapter 26, the capstone of Leviticus (the book explaining the tabernacle service) makes this abundantly clear. It starts by pointing out the benefits accruing to Israel through obedience to God:

> If you walk in My statutes and keep My commandments so as to carry them out, then I shall give you rains in their season, so that the land will yield its produce and the trees of the field will bear their fruit. Indeed, your threshing will last for you until grape gathering, and grape gathering will last until sowing time. You will thus eat your food to the full and live securely in your land. I shall also grant peace in the land, so that you may lie down with no one making you tremble. I shall also eliminate harmful

---

[39] Morales, *Who Shall Ascend the Mountain of the Lord,* p. 106.

beasts from the land, and no sword will pass through your land. But you will chase your enemies, and they will fall before you by the sword; five of you will chase a hundred, and a hundred of you will chase ten thousand, and your enemies will fall before you by the sword. So I will turn toward you and make you fruitful and multiply you, and I will confirm My covenant with you. And you will eat the old supply and clear out the old because of the new. Moreover, I will make My dwelling among you, and My soul will not reject you. I will also walk among you and be your God, and you shall be My people. I am the Lord your God, who brought you out of the land of Egypt so that you should not be their slaves, and I broke the bars of your yoke and made you walk erect (vv. 3–13).

The list of specific blessings here is mind-boggling. Everything from favorable weather to farm production to national security and success in war to noble, upright freedom, all given in order to provide confirmation of the covenant; here we have before us the fulfillment of the command of Gen. 1 to be fruitful, multiply, fill the earth and subdue it. Note also that the command in Gen. 1: 26 and 28, to rule over the animal kingdom, is likewise fulfilled, in particular in the elimination of those darlings of the environmentalist movement, harmful beasts. This of course runs against the grain of their narrative; but the chapter doesn't stop there, as will become evident.

For disobedience has its consequences as well.

But if you do not obey Me and do not carry out all these commandments, if, instead, you reject My statutes, and if your soul abhors My ordinances so as not to carry out all My commandments, and so break My covenant, I, in turn, will do this to you: I will appoint over you a sudden terror, consumption and fever that shall waste away the eyes and cause the soul to pine away; also, you shall sow your seed uselessly, for your enemies shall eat it up. And I will set My face against you so that you shall be struck down before your enemies; and those who hate you shall rule over you, and you shall flee when no one is pursuing you. If also after these things, you do not obey Me, then I will punish you seven times more for your sins. And I will also break down your pride of power; I will also make your sky like iron and your earth like bronze. And your strength shall be spent uselessly, for your land shall not yield its produce and the trees of the land shall not yield their fruit (vv. 14–20).

Here it is mainly failure in warfare that is spoken of, but environmental effects of disobedience to God's law are also indicated. The sky like iron, the earth like bronze – not climate change but God's curse bringing drought, entailing failure in agriculture and fruticulture.

But that is not all.

If then, you act with hostility against Me and are unwilling to obey Me, I will increase the plague on you seven times according to your sins. And I will let loose among you the beasts of the field, which shall bereave you of your children and destroy your cattle and reduce your number so that your roads lie deserted (vv. 21–22).

The return of the wild beasts! Yes, the environmentalist dream scenario once again lived out, although with the unfortunate side effect of dead children and livestock.[40] This will come about not because of abusive land management policies but simply because of disobedience to God's moral laws, as outlined in the earlier chapters of Leviticus, beginning with sexual immorality (chs. 18, 20). But there is more.

And if by these things you are not turned to Me, but act with hostility against Me, then I will act with hostility against you; and I, even I, will strike you seven times for your sins. I will also bring upon you a sword which will execute vengeance for the covenant; and when you gather together into your cities, I will send pestilence among you, so that you shall be delivered into enemy hands. When I break your staff of bread, ten women will bake your bread in one oven, and they will bring back your

---

[40] "What Scripture consistently treats as a curse is the romantic dream of much of the environmentalist movement.... That language is enough to make leaders of the Sierra Club, or the Wilderness Society, or the National Wildlife Foundation, or the World Wildlife Fund, or Earth First!, or any of a score of other environmentalist organizations wax rhapsodic in wistful longing." Beisner, *Where Garden Meets Wilderness*, p. 120.

bread in rationed amounts, so that you will eat and not be satisfied (vv. 23–26).

Pestilence and famine! Again, not because of climate change but part and parcel with defeat in battle, as God avenges Himself for disobedience to His law. And then:

> Yet if in spite of this, you do not obey Me, but act with hostility against Me, then I will act with wrathful hostility against you; and I, even I, will punish you seven times for your sins. Further, you shall eat the flesh of your sons and the flesh of your daughters you shall eat. I then will destroy your high places, and cut down your incense altars, and heap your remains on the remains of your idols; for My soul shall abhor you. I will lay waste your cities as well, and will make your sanctuaries desolate; and I will not smell your soothing aromas (vv. 27–31).

Famine so dreadful that cannibalism results. And even worse – cannibalism of one's own offspring. This in repayment of the idolatry whereby the apotheosized creatures of the natural world are worshipped while the God who created them is spurned.

The result of all of this is Sabbath rest for the land.

> And I will make the land desolate so that your enemies who settle in it shall be appalled over it. You, however, I will scatter among the nations and will draw out a sword after you, as your land becomes desolate and your cities become waste. Then the land will enjoy its sabbaths all the days of the desolation, while you are in your enemies' land; then the land will rest and enjoy its sabbaths (vv. 27–34).

We encounter here an explanation of Sabbath rest for the land which is *utterly at odds* with the explanation provided by our Christian environmentalists. As we saw earlier (p. 11), they argue that the Sabbath rest given by God to the land, when the Babylonians took the Israelites into captivity, was given because the Israelites did not practice proper land management, but instead treated the land exploitatively. Yet when we examine the actual reason for the land's 70-year Sabbath rest, we find that it has absolutely nothing to do with land management, but everything to do with idolatry and immorality.

Chapter 18 makes this clear. The focus there (vv. 6–23) is on sexual immorality. And the price to pay is severe:

> Do not defile yourselves by any of these things; for by all these the nations which I am casting out before you have become defiled. *For the land has become defiled*, therefore I have visited its punishment upon it, *so the land has spewed out its inhabitants.* But as for you, you are to keep My statutes and My judgments, and shall not do any of these abominations, neither the native, nor the alien who sojourns among you (for the men of the land who have been before you have done all these abominations, and *the land has become defiled); so* that the land may not spew you out, should you defile it, as it has spewed out the nation which has been before you (vv. 24–28, emphasis added).

It is not abusive land practices that the land cannot bear, but sexual immorality and attendant child sacrifice (v. 21). It is so unbearable that the land vomits out the practitioners. This, of course, is the last thing modern men and women, even modern Christians, want to hear. It is much more comfortable, much more sensitive, to blame everything on things like abusive land practices. But the land itself begs to differ. It cannot bear with man's violations of God's law. Meanwhile, such a Sabbath rest for the land is anything but a return to Paradise. For such a rest leaves the land so desolate that even the enemies of Israel who resettle it are appalled over it (26: 32).

Isaiah 24

Moving to the other verses adduced in favor of the land-despoliation thesis, what can we say of vv. 4–6 of Isaiah ch. 24? As we have seen, these verses are cited to substantiate God's environmental concern; they are seen as an example of God's judgment upon those who would abuse the good creation. But it is selective citation that suggests such a picture. Verses 1–3 provide some needed context: "Behold, the LORD lays the earth waste, devastates it, distorts its surface, and scatters its inhabitants.... The earth will be completely laid waste and completely despoiled, for the Lord has spoken this word." It is *God* who lays waste to the earth and devastates it. And why does He do so? Because the inhabitants "polluted" the earth by transgressing laws, violating statutes, and breaking the everlasting covenant (v. 5) – in short, for breaking His law. This pollution, then, is not physical but moral.

These other verses make the same point:

Numbers 35: 33: "So you shall not pollute the land in which you are; for blood pollutes the land and no expiation can be made for the land for the blood that is shed on it, except by the blood of him who shed it."

Psalm 106: 38: "... and shed innocent blood, the blood of their sons and their daughters, whom they sacrificed to the idols of Canaan; and the land was polluted with the blood."

Jeremiah 3: 1, 2, 9: "God says, 'If a husband divorces his wife, and she goes from him, and belongs to another man, will he still return to her? Will not that land be completely polluted? But you are a harlot with many lovers; yet you turn to Me,' declares the LORD. 'Lift up your eyes to the bare heights and see; where have you not been violated? By the roads you have sat for them like an Arab in the desert, and you have polluted a land with your harlotry and with your wickedness.'... And it came about because of the lightness of her harlotry, that she polluted the land and committed adultery with stones and trees."

Jeremiah 23: 11: "'For both prophet and priest are polluted; even in My house I have found their wickedness,' declares the LORD."

Micah 4: 11: "And now many nations have been assembled against you who say, 'Let her be polluted, and let our eyes gloat over Zion.'"

Hosea 4

Another verse offered to suggest man-made environmental degradation is Hosea 4: 3: "Therefore the land mourns, and everyone who lives in it languishes along with the beasts of the field and the birds of the sky; and also the fish of the sea disappear." Here again it is context that matters. The previous verses (1–2) provide it: "Listen to the word of the LORD, O sons of Israel, for the Lord has a case against the inhabitants of the land, because there is no faithfulness or kindness or knowledge of God in the land. There is swearing, deception, murder, stealing, and adultery. They employ violence, so that bloodshed follows bloodshed." Here again, there is no mention of abusive land use practices, but only of immorality and criminality, blatant violations of God's law.

The passage continues: "My people are destroyed for lack of knowledge. Because you have rejected knowledge, I also will reject you from being My priest. Since you have forgotten the law of your God, I also will forget your children" (v. 6). Is this not the judgment that awaits us when we abuse, not the land, but God's Word to fit our agendas?

Revelation 11

Finally, Revelation 11: 18, which Van Dyke et al. claim to speak of punishment for those who despoil the natural world – something which, they say, God considers to be "an extreme sin" (see p. 12 above). And of which Hyneman and Shore on behalf of World Vision write: "It is not just those who maliciously mistreat the earth for selfish gain who will be punished, but also those who stand idly by and remain silent about environmental abuses."[41]

This, then, is serious business. How does the verse actually read? "And the nations were enraged, and Thy wrath came, and the time came for the dead to be judged, and the time to give their reward to Thy bond-servants the prophets and to the saints and to those who fear Thy name, the small and the great, and to destroy those who destroy the earth." The word for "destroy" here is *diaphtheirō*, which is a combination of *dia* (thoroughly) and a form of the same word we encountered previously, *phthora* (corruption). It can mean "destroy" or "ruin," and it can also mean to thoroughly corrupt. John uses the same word for two different meanings here, as explained in Ellicott's commentary (*A Bible Commentary for English Readers*): "It is, then, woe on all those who have misused God's gifts and those beautiful things which He gave us liberally to enjoy. It is a woe on those who have defiled those bodies, which are the temples of the Holy Ghost, profaned the earth, which is God's footstool, or darkened by their evil deeds the heaven, which is His throne. Those who thus defile (or, *destroy*: the word is so in the margin, and is the same as that which follows) God's temple anywhere, God will destroy (1 Corinthians 6: 19; 1 Corinthians

---

[41] Hyneman and Shore, *Why are We Stewards of Creation?*, p. 12.

3: 17)."

Other commentaries follow suit:

Matthew Poole (*Annotations upon the Holy Bible*): "the time also is come, when thou hast destroyed, or wilt destroy, that antichristian brood, which so long hath plagued the earth, and destroyed thy people in it."

The Pulpit Commentary: "The wicked are those who 'destroy the earth,' since it is on their account that the world is destroyed; they 'destroy the earth' also by corrupting it, which is the force of διαφθεῖραι [diaphtheirai]."

Barnes (*Notes Explanatory and Practical on the Book of Revelation*): "All who have, in their conquests, spread desolation over the earth and who have persecuted the righteous, and all who have done injustice and wrong to any class of people."

Gill (*Exposition of the Entire Bible*): "And shouldest destroy them which destroy the earth; or 'corrupt it'; meaning antichrist and his followers; who destroy the bodies, souls, and estates of men, and not only the inhabitants of the earth, but even the earth itself; for through that laziness and idleness which they spread wherever they come, a fruitful country is turned into barrenness; who corrupt the minds of men with false doctrine, idolatry, and superstition, and the bodies of women and men with all uncleanness and filthiness, with fornication, sodomy, &c. Revelation 19:2; and are the cause of their own destruction, and the destruction of others; which, upon the blowing of the seventh trumpet, will come swiftly and irrecoverably."

It is thus not environmental degradation which is in view here but, once again, disobedience to God's law, and more specifically the corruption and persecution of the body of Christ, the church. It is a description of the final judgment that will be meted out to sinners, at the same time that reward will be meted out to the obedient.

By this point the misinterpretations and misrepresentations of Scripture on the part of Christian environmentalists should be obvious. It is difficult to avoid the conclusion that for these persons, the agenda is more important than the truth. Scripture will be made to fit the narrative, come what may. But what is this other than the practice of which Jesus convicted the Pharisees when He said to them, "You nicely set aside the com-

mandment of God in order to keep your tradition" (Mark 7: 9)?[42]
Beisner drives the point home:

> By all means let us teach man's accountability to God for his dominion
> over the earth. Let us develop and teach sound principles of resource use
> and conservation, of pollution abatement, of recycling. Let us recognize
> that Scripture reveals environmental consequences of sin. But first and
> foremost, let us call mankind to repentance for sin and faithful obedience
> to God according to His laws, and let us be careful not to read environ-
> mental degradation into passages of Scripture that talk instead of idola-
> try, spiritual adultery, and other such sins that may be committed just as
> much by someone who uses best available practices in soil conservation
> or waste disposal and recycling as by someone who ignores or flouts such
> wise methods.[43]

---

[42] Granberg-Michaelson (*Ecology and Life,* pp. 57ff.) attempts a more nuanced
approach. He quotes Jeremiah 2: 7: "And I brought you into the fruitful land,
to eat its fruit and its good things. But you came and defiled My land...." But
here again the context is determinative. It shows that Israel's transgression is not
against the land but against God. "Has a nation changed gods, when they were
not gods? But My people have changed their glory for that which does not
profit" (v. 11). Recognizing this, Granberg-Michaelson still tries to make land
abuse the issue. "This is one of numerous biblical references portraying the un-
faithfulness and sins of humanity expressed in the destruction of the environment. Yet, this relationship is more profound. Biblical passages frequently suggest that humanity's rebellion against God in any number of ways results in the
land itself suffering, mourning, and becoming unfruitful" (pp. 57–58). Indeed.
But this "suffering" of the land is from God's hand, not man's. Furthermore, it is
not the *reason* for punishment, it *is* the punishment.
[43] *Where Garden Meets Wilderness,* p. 49.

THE MEANING OF STEWARDSHIP

Given this understanding of these key passages of Scripture, we can now come to grips with the concept of stewardship. Christian environmentalists have embraced the idea that human beings are stewards of the natural environment. The document on this subject published by World Vision, entitled *Why Are We Stewards of Creation? World Vision's Biblical Understanding of How We Relate to Creation,* provides a relatively concise summary statement. They write:

> We understand stewardship to be the directive from God to work, care, watch over, guard and protect all that which is entrusted to us.
>
> As World Vision's core value states, 'We are stewards' – resources at our disposal are not our own. We understand our call to stewardship through our study of Genesis 2:15, 'The Lord God took the man and put him in the Garden of Eden to work it and take care of it'.
>
> The Hebrew word for 'care' is *shamar*, meaning to 'watch, guard, protect'. The concept denotes careful and close observation – specifically, an attentive and protective tending.
>
> Genesis 2:15 reveals that creation is to be worked, that humans are created to be workers, that work is the plan of God and not a curse, and that humanity is to be provided for through creation. This passage also shows that, even before the fall, the creation needed to be cared for. This aspect of caring for creation means we are to guard, nurture and protect creation – a good articulation of roles of a steward or servant.
>
> If dominion is responsibility to care for creation, then stewardship describes how we exercise this dominion.
>
> We govern creation for the good of humanity and other parts of creation, not in a domineering, selfish and exploitive manner, but by nurturing creation, preserving it and helping it to function as God intended.
>
> The Bible says God's intention is that humans exercise dominion best by adopting the approach of being stewards – appointed caretakers who follow instructions from God the owner – over creation. Stewardship is

how we exercise dominion as God intends.[44]

The concept of stewardship put forward here perpetuates the misunderstanding we have already highlighted. It speaks of "the directive from God to work, care, watch over, guard and protect all that which is entrusted to us" – but who exactly "us" is, is left undefined. We will return to this. Furthermore, once again the key proof text it adduces is Genesis 2: 15: "We understand our call to stewardship through our study of Genesis 2: 15, 'The Lord God took the man and put him in the Garden of Eden to work it and take care of it'.... Genesis 2: 15 reveals that creation is to be worked, that humans are created to be workers, that work is the plan of God and not a curse, and that humanity is to be provided for through creation." But as we have seen, Gen. 2: 15 has nothing to do with care and nurture of the creation! The reverse is the case. It has to do with guarding and protecting Eden *from* the creation. It has to do with serving in and guarding the temple – which is what the Garden of Eden was.

If Genesis 2: 15 does not speak to stewardship of creation, then which passage of Scripture does? First of all, there is the dominion mandate, in which mankind is called to multiply and fill the earth, to subdue it, and to rule over the animal world. The word for subdue is *kabash*, which according to Strong's Concordance means to bring into bondage. An example of the way this word is used is in Nehemiah 5: 5 (BSB): "We and our children are just like our countrymen and their children, yet we are *subjecting* our sons and daughters to slavery. Some of our daughters are already *enslaved*, but we are powerless to redeem them because our fields and vineyards belong to others." The words in italics are forms of *kabash*.

Another such passage is to be found in Numbers 32: "So Moses said to them, 'If you will do this, if you will arm yourselves before the LORD for the war, and all of you armed men cross over the Jordan before the LORD until He has driven His enemies out from before Him, and the land is subdued before the LORD, then afterward you shall return and be free of obligation toward the LORD and toward Israel, and this land shall be yours for a possession before the LORD'" (vv. 20–22). Subduing the land here is removing the Canaanites – the idolators and the immoral – and so cleansing the land of sin, to prepare it for God's presence. Here is

---

[44] Hyneman and Shore, *Why are We Stewards of Creation?*, p. 20.

another indication that the purpose of Genesis 1–2 is not concerned with how we care for creation, but how we are to prepare the land for the coming of the Lord. The focus is not nature, but God.

This is further emphasized by the other command given by God to man in Gen. 1, to rule over the animal world. The word for rule is *radah,* which Strong's defines as to have dominion, to rule, to dominate. It is mainly used to describe rule over other men, and so describes political rule; it can also refer to the treatment of slaves, as in Leviticus 25: 39–55.

But in Gen. 1 *radah* describes how animals are to be treated. The question then arises, why resort to this language of subjugation and domination? Especially in view of the received understanding that the natural world was created pristine, perfect, and unsullied – what is the point of subjugation and domineering rule? Indeed, it makes no sense in terms of the received understanding. But as we have seen, the received understanding is wrong. And when we understand the creation not to be unspoiled but instead to be subjected to futility and in bondage to corruption *from the beginning,* then this language makes perfect sense. The natural world needed to be brought into subjection, needed to be subjugated, in order to prepare the way for the Lord, such as He presented Himself in Eden. For the perishable cannot inherit the imperishable.[45]

---

[45] This informs us as to how to interpret Gen. 1: 29–30: "Then God said, 'Behold, I have given you every plant yielding seed that is on the surface of all the earth, and every tree which has fruit yielding seed; it shall be food for you; and to every beast of the earth and to every bird of the sky and to every thing that moves on the earth which has life, I have given every green plant for food'; and it was so." Within the framework of understanding we put forward here, this is not a descriptive statement but a prescriptive one. Most commentators agree that this does not rule out meat-eating on the part of man, in view of the skins God clothed Adam and Eve in (requiring the death of the animal), the sacrifice offered by Abel (in which as part of the ritual the meat would be eaten), and the fact that for the purpose of sacrifice Noah separated animals into clean and unclean (Gen. 7: 2). And natural science tells us that ecosystems as currently configured would require an entirely new creation. Therefore, as a descriptive state-

Stewardship of the natural creation is therefore not what is being discussed in Gen. 1–2. This is not to say that there is no concept of stewardship in the Bible. There is. But it has a specific, delimited content which does not answer to the expansive role ascribed to it in modern environmentalist treatments, Christian or otherwise.

Stewardship in the Bible

What is the Scriptural doctrine of stewardship? Hall has this to say: "The Bible as a whole, New as well as Old Testament, contains some twenty-six direct references to the steward and stewardship. The usage of the term in the Hebrew Scriptures is uniformly technical or literal; that is, it describes an actual office or vocation in society."[46] Specifically, it refers to the manager of a household, royal or otherwise. Examples include Eliezer of Damascus, (Abraham's steward), Joseph (Potiphar and Pharaoh), and Shebna (Hezekiah).

In the New Testament, two words are used for steward: *epitropos* and *oikonomos,* both of which refer to a position in a household, the former more in terms of guardianship of persons, the latter (from which we derive the word "economy") having to do with property. As such, stewardship is a function of property and ownership. It is a role delimited by the institutions of family and property.

What about metaphorical usage? There are instances of this as well, and they are telling. Stewardship is applied to officeholders in the church (1 Corinthians 4: 1–2; Titus 1: 7) and to Christians generally in the church (1 Peter 4: 10). This dovetails nicely with our understanding of Gen. 2: 15 as referring to temple service. Our stewardship (temple service

---

ment it fails. But as a prescriptive statement it makes perfect sense. As part of Adam's calling to exercise dominion by extending the Garden-Temple, this would mean an invasion of the ecological world, transforming it into a world no longer exhibiting death, predation, scavenging, etc. Such would fulfill passages such as Isaiah 65: 25: "'The wolf and the lamb shall graze together, and the lion shall eat straw like the ox; and dust shall be the serpent's food. They shall do no evil or harm in all My holy mountain,' says the LORD." How exactly this could come about is of course a matter of pure speculation.

[46] Hall, *The Steward,* pp. 31–32.

and guardianship) is conducted in the church, the household of God (1 Timothy 3: 15); it is our service in God's temple (1 Corinthians 3: 16, 2 Corinthians 6: 16, Ephesians 2: 21).

Where then is the broad concept of stewardship by which mankind is called to practice a sort of universal collective management over the entire planet? In Scripture it is nowhere to be found. Scholars who examine the issue acknowledge that the concept of stewardship in this all-embracing sense is an innovation. Hall writes that the 20th-century North American church originally understood stewardship in a narrow sense, as concerning the collection and administration of church funds, while in Europe the concept was not even broached; only lately has it become current in the broad sense of global management.[47]

The foremost scholar attending to the concept of stewardship, John Reumann, paints a similar picture. Writing in 1992, Reumann discussed his 40 years of investigating the usage of the term stewardship in the Bible and the church. Already back in 1957 he had completed his doctoral dissertation on the word *oikonomia* and related terms.[48] He is unconvinced of the use to which Hall and others have seen fit to put this word.

> Defined as Douglas John Hall would have it, stewardship is a biblical symbol that has come of age only in North America. Even the New Testament never quite got it right. It means care of the globe, together with all right-minded, ecologically inclined people, and correct political action for the future of society. The price for such a definition is to write off almost all church history and presumably most theologizing from Constantine the Great until contemporary liberation theology and seemingly to give up evangelism, which converts people to Jesus Christ, as presumptuous.[49]

Stewardship... or Empire?

Reumann's reticence is well-grounded. The Bible does not speak of

---

[47] Hall, *The Steward*, pp. 3ff.
[48] Reumann, *Stewardship and the Economy of God*, p. 14.
[49] Reumann, *Stewardship and the Economy of God*, p. 63.

stewardship in this manner. But it does have something to say about the presumed management of the earth. And this goes back to the book of Genesis as well.

To understand this, we have to take another look at what was going on in Eden. The twofold vocation given Adam by God can be characterized as priestly and royal.[50] In combining these two offices, Adam was in possession of capacities that we can only dream of. His naming of the animals was echoed in Solomon's kingly vocation.[51] "And God gave Solomon wisdom, exceedingly deep insight, and understanding beyond measure, like the sand on the seashore.... [Solomon] spoke of trees, from the cedar in Lebanon to the hyssop growing in the wall, and he taught about animals, birds, reptiles, and fish. So men of all nations came to listen to Solomon's wisdom, sent by all the kings of the earth, who had heard of his wisdom" (1 Kings 4: 29, 32–34). This was but a portion of what Adam possessed. Not coincidentally, Solomon is the one who built the temple, putting Eden on a permanent footing, so that God would dwell permanently in Jerusalem, thus bringing abundant blessing, including wealth beyond belief (1 Kings 10).

Solomon's wisdom, wealth, power, and dominion provide a hint of the power and wealth that originally was at Adam's command by virtue of his twofold vocation. This is also reflected in the curious passage about the king of Tyre as recounted in Ezekiel ch. 28. This king had attained a level of wealth and power that recalled the original condition in Eden.

---

[50] "Adam should always best be referred to as a 'priest-king', since it is only after the 'fall' that priesthood is separated from kingship, though Israel's eschatological expectation is of a messianic priest-king (e.g., see Zech. 6:12–13)." Beale, *The Temple and the Church's Mission*, p. 70.

[51] "God brought to Adam the birds and beasts to see what he would call them (Gen 2: 19). Man's interpretive role would become of increasing practical importance as an instrument for gaining mastery of the earth in fulfillment of his cultural task, for more and more man's growing knowledge of his world would be the key to his power over it. Stated in terms of cultural office, man's interpretive vocation was a call to the post of wise man-philosopher-scientist. This was not so much an office in itself as it was an adjunct of man's kingship." Kline, *Kingdom Prologue*, pp. 87–88.

You were the seal of perfection,
full of wisdom and perfect in beauty.
You were in Eden,
the garden of God.
Every kind of precious stone adorned you:
ruby, topaz, and diamond,
beryl, onyx, and jasper,
sapphire, turquoise, and emerald.
Your mountings and settings were crafted in gold,
prepared on the day of your creation.
You were anointed as a guardian cherub,
for I had ordained you.
You were on the holy mountain of God;
you walked among the fiery stones.
From the day you were created
you were blameless in your ways—
until wickedness was found in you (vv. 12–15, BSB).

This is quite a remarkable description, providing further details regarding the priestly status of the inhabitant of Eden. For example, the gems it mentions are the same as those which adorned the high priest in the temple, while the reference to the "guardian cherub" highlights the task of temple guardianship.

His fall, as a result of the wickedness found in him, is also mentioned:

By the vastness of your trade,
you were filled with violence, and you sinned.
So I drove you in disgrace
from the mountain of God,
and I banished you, O guardian cherub,
from among the fiery stones.
Your heart grew proud of your beauty;
you corrupted your wisdom because of your splendor;
so I cast you to the earth;
I made you a spectacle before kings (vv. 16–17, BSB).

Sounds like a mercantile Adam, doesn't it? This passage, referring as it does to the king of Tyre, conflates the Edenic status with the worldly situation of this merchant prince, who ruled the waves and exercised dominion over cities and kingdoms by virtue of the power derived from wealth. What is of especial interest here is that Hiram, the original king of Tyre in the Bible, was the great friend of Solomon and provided essential services toward the building of the temple in Jerusalem. In fact, just this is described in the chapter of 1 Kings which immediately follows the passage quoted above. It can be surmised that all the references to Edenic blessing allude to the blessings flowing out of Hiram's proximity to the temple; this blessing fueled the growth of Tyre's trading empire, by which it became a world power.

What does all of this mean? Among other things, this: Adam in the Garden of Eden was not a primitive innocent, but a man of wisdom, wealth, and power, exercising his vocation as king and priest – king over the rest of creation, priest of the Most High God. And the one fed into the other.

But with Adam's fall came the severing of the twofold vocation. The dominion mandate was sundered from the temple service. Instead of exercising guardianship over the temple, Adam was driven away from the temple, his task passed on to the guardian cherubs. And because of this, dominion over the creation became a matter of toil by the sweat of his brow.

Adam's descendants felt the loss keenly. This is reflected in Lamech's plaintive hope expressed at the birth of his son Noah: "May this one comfort us in the labor and toil of our hands caused by the ground that the Lord has cursed" (Gen. 5: 29). Noah's re-establishment of the dominion mandate after the Flood provided some relief, but no essential change.[52] In fact, at this point the fear of man was put into the animal kingdom that did not exist before.

What happened next is of crucial importance to understand all subse-

---

[52] Speaking of Gen. 8: 21, Dumbrell writes, "God will never again curse the ground as he had done in the flood. The verse implies no more than that while the present sinful conduct of human beings will continue in a re-established world, God will take no more action. The issue here is not the removal of the curses of Genesis 3:14–19. They remain." *Covenant and Creation*, p. 93.

quent history. Mankind decided to Babel.[53]

The Response of Babel

Once again, our understanding of this defining moment in history is clouded and truncated by our lack of understanding of what the Garden of Eden was all about. Once we understand that the Garden of Eden, far from being a sort of petting zoo, was the Palatinate, the capital of the world, the residence of God Himself, out of which power extended to the as-yet-unconquered, unsubdued frontier (which is what the rest of the world was), then we can also understand mankind's desire to recapture it.

The Garden of Eden was situated in mountainous terrain, perhaps atop a mountain, thus serving as the model for future holy mountains such as Sinai and Zion. It was luxuriantly verdant, and harbored all manner of precious gems. It had at its disposal the gold and bdellium of Havilah. Flowing through it were the rivers that watered the world. And it had God. This was power, this was wealth, this was beauty.

And ever since Eden, mankind has wished to return. In a letter to his son Christopher, J. R. R. Tolkien gave touching expression to this sentiment:

> Certainly there was an Eden on this very unhappy earth. We all long for it, and we are constantly glimpsing it: our whole nature at its best and least corrupted, its gentlest and most humane, is still soaked with the sense of 'exile'. If you come to think of it, your (very just) horror at the stupid murder of the hawk, and your obstinate memory of this 'home' of yours in an idyllic hour (when often there is an illusion of the stay of time and decay and a sense of gentle peace)... are derived from Eden. As far as we can go back the nobler part of the human mind is filled with the thoughts of *sibb*, peace and goodwill, and with the thought of its *loss*. We shall never recover it, for that is not the way of repentance, which works

---

[53] "Man calls his projected city Bab-el, *the gate*—that is, the court—*of God;* God calls it Babble; for in all languages indistinct and confused speech is represented by the action of the lips in producing the sound of *b*." Ellicott (ed.), *An Old Testament Commentary for English Readers*, vol. 1, p. 54.

spirally and not in a closed circle; we may recover something like it, but on a higher plane.[54]

Beale and Kim speak in a similar vein. Inspired by this statement of Tolkien's, they write:

We are creatures of longing. When we misdiagnose the object of this longing, then we become frustrated and disappointed. Our longings for relationship often get frustrated in conflict. Our longings for satisfaction get frustrated in discontent. Our longings for significance get frustrated by our own inadequacies. J. R. R. Tolkien diagnoses the roots of our long- ing.... The longings of our hearts are frustrated from this exile, but these longings are properly satisfied in the dwelling place of God originally found in Eden.[55]

This is the explicit or implicit theme of novels become movies like *Lost Horizon* (James Hilton, 1933), of pop songs like "Woodstock" (Joni Mitchell) and "Been to Canaan" (Carole King) and "Saturday in the Park" (Chicago).

But as with those human representations, it is always accomplished on man's own terms. This is what mankind has wished for ever since his fall and banishment. And it is what explains the tower of Babel.

The actual happening is summed up in surprisingly few verses:

Now the whole earth used the same language and the same words. And it came about as they journeyed east, that they found a plain in the land of Shinar and settled there. And they said to one another, "Come, let us make bricks and burn them thoroughly." And they used brick for stone, and they used tar for mortar. And they said, "Come, let us build for our- selves a city, and a tower whose top will reach into heaven, and let us make for ourselves a name; lest we be scattered abroad over the face of the whole earth" (Gen. 11: 1–4).

Recall that this event followed upon the flood. Prior to it, Eden still

---

[54] *The Letters of J. R. R. Tolkien*, p. 110.
[55] *God Dwells Among Us*, p. 17.

existed, and mankind could still approach Eden from the east (e.g., Gen. 4: 16); afterward, Eden was no longer to be found. The center of gravity was gone. Without it, mankind wandered eastward and began to disperse. But the more enterprising among them realized that they might attempt to recapture Eden if they stuck together and pitched in. They decided on a self-made mountain. In this way they could recreate the original condition, but on their own terms, using bricks which they themselves made; by their own efforts they would force their way into God's presence and so gain His blessing. Jesus would later speak of this mindset: "And from the days of John the Baptist until now the kingdom of heaven suffers violence, and violent men take it by force" (Matthew 11: 12). And in this way, they would make a name for themselves, for having struck out on their own, they no longer waited upon the name of the Lord. "I have come in My Father's name, and you do not receive Me; if another shall come in his own name, you will receive him" (John 5: 43). As Alexander puts it, "what we have here is an account in which all the God-given abilities of human beings are deliberately focused on creating a society where God is redundant. Confident in their own capacity to meet every challenge, the inhabitants of this human city view the Creator as irrelevant."[56]

The result of this endeavor was not the recapture of Eden but the confusion of languages, the formation of separate nations, and the hostility of nations to one another. And it precipitated yet another momentous development – idolatry and worship of nature. For it is only from this time forward that we hear of such. Apparently, the confusion of language likewise brought about a confusion of mind. "For even though they knew God, they did not honor Him as God, or give thanks; but they became futile in their speculations, and their foolish heart was darkened." This result was an inversion of Creator and creature: "Professing to be wise, they became fools, and exchanged the glory of the incorruptible God for an image in the form of corruptible man and of birds and four-footed animals and crawling creatures" (Romans 1: 21–23).

Man's attempt to recover the lost Adamic priesthood was repaid by allowing him to establish priesthoods in the service of "birds and four-

---

[56] *From Eden to the New Jerusalem*, p. 28.

footed animals and crawling creatures." No longer could man properly represent God to himself. He began to make, and serve, images of the things he was supposed to rule over: "You shall not make for yourself an idol, or any likeness of what is in heaven above or on the earth beneath, or in the water under the earth. You shall not worship them nor serve them" (Exodus 20: 4–5).[57] The loss of dominion now translated itself into the service of that of which he should be master.

How much of environmentalism is merely an updated version of this selfsame phenomenon?

The era had now dawned of which Paul spoke in Acts 14: "We are also men, of the same nature as you, preaching the gospel to you, to turn from these useless things to a living God, who made the heaven and the earth and the sea, and everything that is in them. In past generations He permitted all the nations to go their own ways; and yet He did not leave Himself without witness...." (vv. 15–16).

And there would be encores of the same Babelic agenda, as nations rose up conquering and to conquer, establishing hegemonic empires, presuming to unite the entire world under one ruler. Unsurprisingly, it would be Babylon that would stand out in this effort – Babylon in fact being the same word as Babel. Isaiah documented the Babylonian attempt to rule the world, a renewed tower of Babel reaching to heaven only to be cast down:

> How you have fallen from heaven,
> You star of the morning, son of the dawn!
> You have been cut down to the earth,
> You who defeated the nations!
> But you said in your heart,

---

[57] The word here translated "serve" is a derivation of *'ābad,* which we also found in Gen. 2: 15 (see p. 10 above). Christian environmentalists tell us that on the basis of Gen. 2: 15 we *should* be serving the creation: "In the eyes of God, the one who rules is the one who serves. So humans are called to rule and subdue the creation by serving it. In fact, the Hebrew phrase of Genesis 2:15, normally translated 'till and keep,' could be as accurately rendered 'serve and preserve.'" (Van Dyke et al., *Redeeming Creation,* pp. 93). But Ex. 20: 5 reserves this service to God; it specifically forbids it to be paid to creatures.

'I will ascend to heaven;
I will raise my throne above the stars of God,
And I will sit on the mount of assembly
In the recesses of the north.
I will ascend above the heights of the clouds;
I will make myself like the Most High.'
Nevertheless you will be brought down to Sheol,
To the recesses of the pit.
Those who see you will stare at you,
They will closely examine you, saying,
'Is this the man who made the earth tremble,
Who shook kingdoms,
Who made the world like a wilderness
And overthrew its cities,
Who did not allow his prisoners to go home?' (14: 12–17)

It is a recurring theme in Scripture and in history, culminating in the vision of Mystery Babylon in the book of Revelation.

This was one agenda mankind would follow. But there was another, initiated by God precisely in response to the Babel episode.

The Response of Abraham

Now Terah took his son Abram, and Lot the son of Haran, his grandson, and his daughter-in-law Sarai, his son Abram's wife, and they departed together from Ur of the Chaldeans to go to the land of Canaan; and they went as far as Haran and settled there.... Now the Lord said to Abram, "Go from your country, and from your relatives and from your father's house, to the land which I will show you; and I will make you into a great nation, and I will bless you, and make your name great; and you shall be a blessing; and I will bless those who bless you, and the one who curses you I will curse. And in you all the families of the earth will be blessed" (Gen. 11: 31, 12: 1–3).

God called Abram out of Babylon, the land of the Chaldeans, into a new land, one which like Eden would flow with milk and honey; He would make him into a great nation; He would make his name great; He would bless him, and channel blessing to the world through him. Point for point He would answer the tower builders, providing in Abram the true return to Eden. "The road from Haran to the land of Canaan symbolizes the return of humanity to Eden and to God. Abraham and the promised land provide the counterpoint and answer to Adam and the Garden of Eden."[58]

Tower of Babel	Call of Abram
"As they journeyed east... they found a plain in the land of Shinar and settled there"	"Go forth from your country to the land I will show you"
"Let us build for ourselves a city"	"I will make you a great nation"
"and a tower whose top will reach into heaven"	"and I will bless you"
"let us make for ourselves a name"	"and make your name great"

The table depicts the autonomous God-dismissing agenda followed by the tower builders, as compared with the responsive God-willed agenda followed by Abram.

In fulfillment of the promise of Gen. 1–2, the covenantal relation established by God with Abram, soon to be *given* the name Abraham ("father of many nations," Gen. 17: 5) embraced 1) land ("fill the earth"), 2) progeny ("be fruitful and multiply"), and 3) the presence of God. "The promise, though repeated and elaborated throughout the patriarchal narratives, contains basically three elements...: posterity, relation with God and the land."[59]

Abram received "independent" confirmation of this promise through the intervention of a mysterious personage who makes his appearance and then vanishes – Melchizedek, "king of righteousness" (Gen. 14: 18–20). This king had his residence in Salem, the location of the later Jerusalem, for which reason the author of the book of Hebrews calls him "king of peace," Salem meaning peace ("shalom"). The interesting thing about Melchizedek is that he was likewise "priest of the Most High God." So

---

[58] Och, "Creation and Redemption," p. 233.

[59] Dyrness, *Let the Earth Rejoice*, p. 49.

then, for the only time prior to the advent of Jesus Christ (who was Himself priest "after the order of Melchizedek," Psalm 110; Hebrews 5, 7), we encounter a single person who embodies the twofold office of priest and king. Melchizedek is therefore a throwback to Adam himself; he makes his appearance in order to bless Abram and, via the Noahic administration, to establish continuity with the original Adamic vocation.

Israel, the nation which descended from Abraham, inherited all of this and put it into practice, favored with the presence of God in the tabernacle and then the temple, receiving His statutes and ordinances, arranging national life in terms of His will, and obtaining His abundant blessing.

THE EFFECT ON NATURE

None of this left the natural world unaffected. For one thing, provisions for the treatment of the natural world were included in the laws handed down by God to Moses and the Israelites.

Biblical Law on the Treatment of Animals

Various laws dealt with the treatment of animals. The Sabbath day provided rest not only for man but for livestock (Ex. 20: 10), while the Sabbath year provided rest for the land, and both domesticated and wild animals could derive nourishment from what grew upon it in that year (Ex. 23: 11; Lev. 25: 2ff.). The mule collapsing under its load should be helped, even if it be the mule of one's enemy (Ex. 23: 5; Deut. 22: 4). An ox or sheep should not be slaughtered together with its offspring (Lev. 22: 28), nor should a young goat be cooked in its mother's milk (Ex. 23: 19, 34: 26; Deut. 14: 21)

There is a clear symbolic, ethical meaning to these laws: they are intended to illustrate and thereby emphasize ethical commands vis-á-vis one's neighbor. In the case of Sabbath rest, it is obvious that livestock could not be worked if human beings were not to work – the one entails the other. Similarly, the rest given the land in the Sabbath year is rest given to human beings who otherwise would have to work the land. Help given to the mule collapsing under its load is a service rendered to the owner, one's neighbor, even though he be an enemy, thus illustrating the command given in Proverbs 25: 21 (and repeated in Rom. 12: 20) to provide one's enemy with food and drink. The commandment not to slaughter parent and offspring together, nor to cook offspring in its mother's milk, inculcates the precept of honoring mother and father by respecting the bond between parent and child.

One text on the treatment of animals deserves special notice. It has already been mentioned (see p. 1): "You shall not muzzle the ox while he is threshing" (Deut. 25: 4). The meaning would seem to be clear – the ox working to prepare grain should be allowed to partake in the product of his labor, and not be prevented by being muzzled. A law which has as its aim the proper treatment of animals by man.

Or so we would think, were it not for the apostle Paul. He quotes this exact verse in his first letter to the Corinthians. "For it is written in the Law of Moses, 'you shall not muzzle the ox while he is threshing.' God is not concerned about oxen, is He? Or is He speaking altogether for our sake? Yes, for our sake it was written, because the plowman ought to plow in hope, and the thresher to thresh in hope of sharing the crops. If we sowed spiritual things in you, is it too much if we should reap material things from you?" (1 Cor. 9: 9–11).

What are we to make of this? For one thing, it proves the point made above, that the laws given for the treatment of animals were not given simply for the animals' sake, but to teach a greater lesson, regarding the treatment of one's neighbor. "Do not fear; you are of more value than many sparrows" (Luke 12: 7). For another, it teaches that the animals which were the subject of these laws, and by extension the natural world, are not ends in themselves, to be treated as a Kantian *Reich der Zwecke;* they were given by God as means to an end, the end of maintaining human society. Human society is built upon the natural world, which is there precisely to enable human society to survive and flourish.

This is the upshot of Breier's observation that "animals appear in ancient law primarily in relation to property law. These regulations—designed to protect an individual's possessions—formed the heart of ancient Near Eastern legal codes."[60] As such, they fall under the regime of biblical stewardship. What, then, does biblical stewardship look like? We will see in the next section.

From Wilderness to Garden

Flourishing nature would be the result if, like Israel, mankind would obey God's law, for then He would dwell in their midst, the result of which would be a thriving bounty, not only for human society but for the natural world as well.

God's presence is the key. If we really wish for a flourishing, bountiful, thriving world of nature, we have to establish His temple in our midst and orient human society around it. Then nature too will rejoice: "The mountains and the hills will break forth into shouts of joy before you, and all

---

[60] Breier, "Animals in Biblical Law and Ancient Near Eastern Law," p. 167.

the trees of the field will clap their hands" (Isaiah 55: 12). *There is no other way.* And why should there be? "God with us" is the goal of history.

We already saw this promised in Lev. 26. Many other verses hold out the same promise. For instance, Isaiah ch. 35:

The wilderness and the desert will be glad,
And the Arabah will rejoice and blossom;
Like the crocus
It will blossom profusely
And rejoice with rejoicing and shout of joy.
The glory of Lebanon will be given to it,
The majesty of Carmel and Sharon.
They will see the glory of the LORD,
The majesty of our God.
[...]

Then the eyes of the blind will be opened,
And the ears of the deaf will be unstopped.
Then the lame will leap like a deer,
And the tongue of the dumb will shout for joy.

For waters will break forth in the wilderness
And streams in the Arabah.
And the scorched land will become a pool,
And the thirsty ground springs of water;
In the haunt of jackals, its resting place,
Grass becomes reeds and rushes.

And a highway will be there, a roadway,
And it will be called the Highway of Holiness.
The unclean will not travel on it,
But it will be for him who walks that way,
And fools will not wander on it.

No lion will be there,

Nor will any vicious beast go up on it;
These will not be found there.
But the redeemed will walk there,
And the ransomed of the LORD will return,
And come with joyful shouting to Zion,
With everlasting joy upon their heads.
They will find gladness and joy,
And sorrow and sighing will flee away.

Once again we notice here that wilderness is to be supplanted by the garden. But this is not just any garden. It is the Garden *of Eden,* thus in fact the place of God's presence. As such, it is God's presence, not mere floral arrangements, that is in view here. And despite the visions of romantic environmentalists, this entails the supplanting of wilderness, including wild animals.

It is instructive in this context to take a look at a set of provisions in the Bible regarding the animal kingdom which is hardly ever brought up in the context of environmental concern, and that is the provisions regarding clean and unclean animals.[61] These provisions are outlined in Leviticus 11 and Deuteronomy 14.

A few interesting points regarding this divine classification:

- Only a few animals are clean, and of those, only a few are fit to be used to approach God (by way of sacrifice).
- Wild animals are for the most part unclean, and never fit to be used to approach God.
- As such, only domesticated animals are worthy of being brought into God's presence.

Now then, if nature untouched by man is pristine and in harmonious balance with itself, why is it that only animals that have been brought under man's dominion and care can be used for sacrifice? Wouldn't that honor fall to the pristine? And why does the Bible (Leviticus 11; Deuteronomy 14) refer to so many animals as abominable and detestable (*šeqeṣ,*

---

[61] The lone exception that I have run across is Block's essay "To Serve and to Keep," which summarizes Leviticus and Deuteronomy with regard to the classification of animals, but neither explains the clean/unclean distinction nor draws conclusions from it.

tôʿēḇâ)?

Apparently pristine is not the appropriate characterization. For contrary to the opinion of many, the Bible harbors no romantic view of wildness or wilderness. On the contrary, it portrays wilderness first as a condition of curse, and then also as God's tool for judgment leading to restoration.

The Call of the Wild

This should come as no surprise, given the understanding of creation such as we gleaned in the earlier discussion. Wilderness, the natural world outside Eden, is "subjected to futility" and in "slavery to corruption" and as such cannot inherit the kingdom of God. It is in need of redemption, which will come finally through the resurrection of the body. In the meantime, it is to be transformed to make way for human settlement. This settlement is to occur roundabout the temple, the dwelling place of God.

This, as we saw, is the message of Leviticus 26. There wilderness is curtailed in favor of agriculture and pasturage, and returns only when God uses it to chastise an unfaithful people. But looked at more closely, wilderness marks the entire history of Israel. The initial exodus out of Egypt meant entry in the wilderness, where God tested Israel's faithfulness. For their part, the Israelites began to express their strong opinion that they would rather have stayed in Egypt than have been led out into this land. Mauser points out the inner conflict: "The constitutive elements of Israel's faith and life are rooted in the wilderness tradition. And yet there is another element in this same tradition marking a glaring contrast to those salutary events—the element of the people's murmuring on the way.... In the course of the long sojourn there is indeed much reason why Yahweh's command to leave Egypt is felt by the wanderers to be an unbearable burden."[62] And Mauser makes a striking observation with regard to the incident of the golden calf: "The bull or calf, the central image of Canaanite worship of fertility, is the representation of the blessings of nature in a land of agriculture. To worship of fertility deities belong public feasting and sexual orgies, a trait displayed in Ex. 32.6. Plainly, the Israelites are

---

[62] Mauser, *Christ in the Wilderness*, p. 29.

tired of the life in the desert; they long for plentiful food and enjoyment."[63] It is the settled, agricultural life which the Israelites longed for; this wilderness experience, as we might say, is "for the birds." They had absolutely no interest in it.

The ultimatum of garden-through-faithfulness versus wilderness-through-unfaithfulness is posed forcefully by Moses in Deuteronomy ch. 8:

> All the commandments that I am commanding you today you shall be careful to do, that you may live and multiply, and go in and possess the land which the LORD swore to give to your forefathers. And you shall remember all the way which the LORD your God has led you in the wilderness these forty years, that He might humble you, testing you, to know what was in your heart, whether you would keep His commandments or not. And He humbled you and let you be hungry, and fed you with manna which you did not know, nor did your fathers know, that He might make you understand that man does not live by bread alone, but man lives by everything that proceeds out of the mouth of the LORD. Your clothing did not wear out on you, nor did your foot swell these forty years. Thus you are to know in your heart that the LORD your God was disciplining you just as a man disciplines his son. Therefore, you shall keep the commandments of the LORD your God, to walk in His ways and to fear Him. For the LORD your God is bringing you into a good land, a land of brooks of water, of fountains and springs, flowing forth in valleys and hills; a land of wheat and barley, of vines and fig trees and pomegranates, a land of olive oil and honey; a land where you shall eat food without scarcity, in which you shall not lack anything; a land whose stones are iron, and out of whose hills you can dig copper. When you have eaten and are satisfied, you shall bless the LORD your God for the good land which He has given you.

The wilderness experience is presented as a period of testing, a necessary step to make Israel fit for its calling as the people of God and the servant of God. The successful completion of the test would result in the fulfilment of the dominion mandate of Gen. 1. And the firstfruits would

---

[63] Mauser, *Christ in the Wilderness*, p. 31.

be returned to God, in thanksgiving for His blessing (cf. Leviticus 23: 9–22).

But self-willed pride and disobedience would be met with a return to "the great and terrible wilderness."

> Beware lest you forget the LORD your God by not keeping His commandments and His ordinances and His statutes which I am commanding you today; lest, when you have eaten and are satisfied, and have built good houses and lived in them, and when your herds and your flocks multiply, and your silver and gold multiply, and all that you have multiplies, then your heart becomes proud, and you forget the LORD your God who brought you out from the land of Egypt, out of the house of slavery. He led you through the great and terrible wilderness, with its fiery serpents and scorpions and thirsty ground where there was no water; He brought water for you out of the rock of flint. In the wilderness He fed you manna which your fathers did not know, that He might humble you and that He might test you, to do good for you in the end. Otherwise, you may say in your heart, 'My power and the strength of my hand made me this wealth.' But you shall remember the LORD your God, for it is He who is giving you power to make wealth, that He may confirm His covenant which He swore to your fathers, as it is this day. And it shall come about if you ever forget the LORD your God, and go after other gods and serve them and worship them, I testify against you today that you shall surely perish. Like the nations that the LORD makes to perish before you, so you shall perish; because you would not listen to the voice of the LORD your God.

This is a comprehensive appraisal of the situation. The Israelites are reminded that through obedience they will "live and multiply" and possess the land, in fulfilment of the dominion mandate. The wilderness experience had been for their own good, to reveal their hearts to themselves. And by leaving behind the wilderness and entering into the promised land, a land which for all intents and purposes was a recovery of Eden, they would enter into the fullness of covenant blessing, a condition characterized by bounteous agricultural and pastoral yields, by which they would become wealthy. But they would also have to guard their hearts to keep from falling into the tower builders' sin and the king of Tyre's sin and the king of Babylon's sin – the pride which says that what they have is of their own making, and not God's, who gives the power to make wealth. For the land itself will respond to that pride by spewing the inhabitants out (cf. Lev. 18: 25, 28) and so revert to wilderness (cf. Lev. 26: 22, 32, 34–35, 43).

BIBLICAL STEWARDSHIP IN HISTORY

What, then, are we to make of the concept of stewardship? Given what the Bible tells us, we have some basic categories within which we need to restrict ourselves if we are to remain faithful to God's Word.

The basic categories are these: the land is to be settled and developed roundabout the temple of God; this is to be conducted on the basis of family and property; the firstfruits of that development are to be offered back to God. This, then, is the truly circular economy, whereby we understand "economy" to be the exercise of *oikonomia*, or stewardship as set forth in Scripture.

What is the temple of God? The temple built by Solomon was destroyed by the Babylonians. The so-called second temple was built upon the return of the Israelites from the Babylonian captivity. It was this temple of which Jesus said, "Destroy this temple, and in three days I will raise it up" (John 2: 19). And indeed this came to pass. The temple was physically destroyed by the Romans, but it had already been spiritually destroyed by the Jews, who had taken the temple, which was to be a house of prayer for all the nations, and turned it into a den of thieves (Matthew 21: 13; Luke 19: 46; cf. Isaiah 56: 7, Jeremiah 7: 11).

The temple of which Jesus spoke when He said He would raise it up in three days, was the temple of His body (John 2: 21). And as we know from, among other places, Paul's first letter to the Corinthians, the body of Christ is the church, believers both individually and corporately (3: 16; 6: 16, 19). The new age is the age in which this temple, the church, spreads throughout the world, whereby the dispersal wrought by the confusion of tongues at Babel is reversed. In principle this already occurred at Pentecost, when the Holy Spirit overcame the language barrier. In this, the temple became the possession not of the Jews alone but of all the nations.

So then, it is roundabout this temple, the church, that the new culture is built, a culture into which the blessing of God, derived from His presence, is channeled.

The history of Western civilization is stamped by this newfound reality. The constituent elements which would form Western society were transformed by it. Let us examine some elements of that process.

The Infrastructure of Western Civilization

In the days when civilization as they knew it was collapsing all around them, Roman Christians did what they knew they must. They gathered together the elements of their culture that were essential to its continuity and deposited them in their Ark of the Covenant. That ark was the monastery.

Monasticism was far more than a simple flight from the world.[64] It was a flight to a new civilization. It signified a total break with a civilization built upon the natural man. It was the embodiment of the living sacrifice, acceptable to God: a renunciation of the world, the flesh, and the Devil, upon which had been built the City of Man; a world which had to be crucified and buried before it could be resurrected.

It was Augustine who, humanly speaking, laid the groundwork for this effort. He more than any other realized how total was the need for the natural man to die, to rise again as a new man through the resurrection power of Christ. And yet he understood that it was not the creation itself, nor the cultural efforts of fallen man, which were evil, but the evil will with which these were infused. Man and his works needed to be purged, not eliminated. This purgation would prove to be salvation; Roman civilization would live on, because it would first die, as it had in this man, this preeminent Roman.

Augustine's attitude to culture was therefore momentously unambiguous. The inheritance of classical civilization could serve the spiritual end of man if it were properly subordinated to that spiritual end. The crown of classical civilization was formed by the *artes liberales,* the Liberal Arts – literally, the arts of freedom. True freedom, Augustine knew only too well, came only in a release from bondage to sin and the flesh. By recasting this inheritance of liberty in terms of the liberty in which Christ sets men free (cf. Ephesians 5:1), this entire civilization could gain a new lease on life.

---

[64] This belies the thesis of Rod Dreher's popular book, *The Benedict Option* (New York: Sentinel, 2017), which for all that does provide bounteous good advice to the modern church. Benedictine monasticism did not withdraw from the world but conquered it, as we shall see.

The process of assimilation of classical culture into the new civilization took place in the monastery. The civilization which had become Christian in name, but remained pagan at heart, underwent a baptism. The monastery reconstructed the material world in terms of the spiritual; it placed the keys of God's kingdom at the center of earthly life. Liturgy was its lifeblood, and from this life flowed the power to purge, renew, and restore the life of this dead civilization.[65]

Cassiodorus, a Roman who spent 40 years of his life in public service to the Gothic king Theodoric, who reigned over the western fragment of the empire, spent the last part of his life gathering together and preserving for posterity the classics, both Christian and pagan, of his dying world. He set aside his patrimonial estate as a monastery, to bring together spiritually-minded brothers and sisters to share in this death-unto-life. He set them upon the task of copying the manuscripts which embodied their civilization. Cassiodorus's innovation initiated the monastic tradition by which the classical Christian inheritance was transmitted to new times and to new stewards.

Cassiodorus's contemporary, Benedict, devised the rule by which Western monasticism would henceforth be governed. Benedict's Rule captured the Roman genius for discipline, order, organization, and practical bent. The Rule was a rule for a common and social life rather than for a life of isolation. Honest labor was established as one of the pillars of a monk's routine. And compared with other monastic rules, it was relatively flexible and mild.

Benedict put worship – the chanting of Psalms, the preaching of God's Word and the celebration of the sacrament – at the center of monastic life. The entire Psalter would be gone through each week; the greater part of the Bible would be read aloud each year.[66] There was obligatory time

---

[65] In his *Liturgy in the Reformed Tradition,* Noordmans notes many points of contact between Roman Catholic and Reformed liturgy, they both being products of the Western, Roman, Augustinian church.

[66] "At the centre of every requirement of the Rule there lies the prescription of a daily round of divine service. For the time at which it was written the regulations for these corporate acts of worship are remarkably careful and unambiguous.

set aside for reading and study, transmitting the sanctified wisdom and culture of the past; it was also obligatory to work, out in the fields or perhaps in the kitchen, on tasks essential to the upkeep of the monastery. Work was necessary; diligence was good for the soul, idleness, the Devil's workshop.

The Rule embodied the kind of rigid discipline which the times required. Every aspect of life was regulated; orders were unquestioningly obeyed. In this manner, stubborn and willful human nature was to be put to death, leaving a humble and submissive spirit, exercised in patience and forbearance. Membership in the monastic community was established by oath, after the model of the Roman legions: these were spiritual warriors, forged into a disciplined fighting machine.

The monasteries were the outposts of civilization in a barbaric world. The world of the laity, of material culture, clustered about them, giving the civilization-in-the-making a new center of gravity. The presence of a monastery sanctified the surrounding countryside, giving spiritual security to a world terrified of roaming devils. Public order arose upon a new spiritual base, purged of the demonic. Consider the importance assigned by contemporaries to a newly-founded abbey:

> The abbot is armed with spiritual weapons and supported by a troop of monks anointed with the dew of heavenly graces. They fight together in the strength of Christ with the sword of the spirit against the aery wiles of the devils. They defend the king and clergy of the realm from the onslaughts of their invisible enemies.[67]

The whole system is built on two biblical pillars: 'at midnight I will rise to give thanks unto thee', and 'seven times a day do I praise thee' – hence the long night-office, and the seven day-offices of Matins (or Lauds), Prime, Terce, Sext, Nones, Vespers, and Compline. The main structure and psalmody are clearly laid out to ensure the weekly recitation of the whole Psalter and the annual reading (much less clearly indicated) of the greater part of the Bible." R.W. Southern, *Western Society and the Church in the Middle Ages*, p. 221.

[67] Foundation charter of King Edgar for New Minster, Winchester, 966, in the *Liber Vitae*, ed. W. de Gray Birch, 1892, pp. 232–46; quoted in Southern, *Western Society and the Church*, pp. 224–225.

The monks of the Dark Ages lived and preached a world-and-life-view radically opposed to the prevailing barbarian culture, but one of which that culture became fascinated and by which it eventually was conquered. Monastic discipline and piety served to demonstrate the demands of the gospel to a culture which knew nothing but blood and honor. The renunciation of the things which that society most valued – territory, kinship, prowess – resulted in the development of a lay piety and ethic which restored these things to their proper role. For example, the ideal of celibacy and the renunciation of the "family values" of the day, the values of a clan society, brought about the transformation of the family. It resulted in the rise of an ethic centered on the nuclear family rather than the clan, upholding the mutual fidelity of husband and wife rather than the loose ethic which permitted adultery and incest and allowed for no family surname because brothers' and sisters' fathers and mothers so often did not coincide. This transformed institution formed the building block of the budding social order of the West.[68]

The monasteries instilled the Augustinian understanding of freedom in barbarian society. In so doing, they made possible the rise of Western civilization. This civilization was built not upon the abstract notion of innate human freedom, but rather on the idea of human corruption, human depravity, and the necessity to submit to God-ordained authority. The truly free man was the man who humbled himself, who recognized his fundamental corruption and bewailed it rather than gloried in it. He was one who could love his enemies, pray for them, and forgive the wrongs done against him. The slave was the man who was enslaved to glory, to vengeance, to mastery. He was caught in a snare of his own device, "for all they that take the sword shall perish with the sword" (Matthew 26: 52). The only reason for the *dominium* of man over man was his own sin. Because man lacked self-control, an external restraint had to be placed upon him. No man was better than another simply because he exercised *dominium* over the other. The slave subject to Christ was the true freeman; the *dominus* wrapped up in his own vices was the true slave. Only grace could restore the condition of self-control, and so the original

---

[68] This development has been brilliantly traced by Georges Duby in *The Knight, the Lady and the Priest.*

condition of man, exercising dominion over the creation rather than over his fellow man.

This was the message brought by the church to a society based on, in Duby's words, "war and slavery."[69] The church held the rulers accountable to a standard of justice consistent with this fallen state. Yes, rulers held a near-absolute authority over their subjects, but to what end? Not to serve their own lusts, but to further the good of those very subjects. Not only that, but it was to their own benefit to grant their subjects as much liberty as they could exercise consistent with the claims of order. The manumission of slaves and serfs was a blessed act. The church, herself a *domina* with slaves and serfs under her control, showed the way here, as witness an act of Gregory the Great:

> Gregory to Montana &c.
>
> Since our Redeemer, the Maker of every creature, vouchsafed to assume human flesh for this end, that, the chain of slavery wherewith we were held being broken by the grace of His Divinity, He might restore us to pristine liberty, it is a salutary deed if men whom nature originally produced free, and whom the law of nations has subjected to the yoke of slavery, be restored by the benefit of manumission to the liberty in which they were born. And so, moved by loving-kindness and by consideration of this case, we make you, Montana and Thomas, servants of the holy Roman church which with the help of God we serve, free from this day, and Roman citizens, and we release to you all your private property.[70]

This was the basis for the growth of constitutional liberties, because it made possible an Augustinian-covenantal progress in liberty.[71] The relationship between ruler and ruled was based on covenant. This was evident in the feudal bond (lord and vassal), the manorial bond (lord and serf), and, later on, in the growth of the cities (city-dwellers and regional

---

[69] Georges Duby, *The Three Orders: Feudal Society Imagined*, p. 150.

[70] Epistle XII, Book VI, *The Book of Pastoral Rule and Selected Epistles of Gregory the Great,* trans. etc. Rev. James Barmby, D.D., in Philip Schaff (ed.), *Nicene and Post-Nicene Fathers,* Second Series, vol. XII, p. 191.

[71] For more on this, see my *Calvin and the Whigs.*

lord). The slave/free dichotomy was eliminated, replaced by a relative hierarchy of freedom: the more freedoms one enjoyed, the more responsibilities he incurred. Serfdom was the lowest rung on this ladder, but even serfs had covenantally-guaranteed rights, focused on family and property.

The church oversaw the covenantal process, ensuring that the rights and duties laid upon both parties were consistent with Augustinian principles of justice. This meant that obedience needed to be rendered to the superior, while a degree of freedom should be granted to the inferior consistent with his ability to exercise that freedom properly. The seal of these covenantal agreements was the oath, sworn to the Holy Trinity. This was the basis for the church's oversight. Through the oath, the superior was bound to keep his agreement with his inferior. Default meant that the inferior was released from his obligation to obedience (in feudal terms, *diffidatio*). Because these agreements were covenantal, they also extended to future generations. They were therefore renewed with each generation. At each renewal ceremony, the stipulations could change by mutual consent, thus allowing for amelioration.

It was the church's oversight which enabled this process to succeed. Apart from her mediation, covenanting parties would be left face-to-face, each determining for himself whether the other party was properly fulfilling the conditions of the covenant. A covenanting process requires a mediator, an arbitrator; otherwise it degenerates to a relationship of force and deceit. And since the covenanting process in the West was conducted under the auspices of the church, in terms of Trinitarian oaths, the eternal destinies of the covenanting parties were implicated. In an age of faith, the threat of eternal sanctions for violation of a sacred oath was enough to deter even the most headstrong.[72]

Liberty grew in fitful stages, as the leaven of freedom on the basis of authority permeated Western society. Western liberty did not exist *a priori*, the patrimony of barbarian (Teutonic, Saxon, Batavian, etc.) tribe culture, a patrimony which was submerged by the church during the Dark Ages only to be recovered after that age expired (a thesis dear to Enlightenment historians, enabling them to avoid having to give the church any

---

[72] Kingship played a complementary role with the church in this process. On this point, see my *A Common Law*, pp. 49ff.

credit for the genesis of their civilization). Through the patient work of
the monks, the heart of European culture was subdued to the claims of
Christ. The institutions which arose – the nuclear family, chivalry
(Burke's "spirit of a gentleman"), the universities, the cities, the free mar-
ket, the rule of law, constitutional government, chartered rights and liberties, even nationhood and international law – all found their roots in
this labor. The monks created European civilization's *true* infrastructure:
the infrastructure of the heart and soul.

The Superstructure of Western Civilization

Such were the foundations of Western Civilization. Erected upon
them came advances in culture that were unprecedented. Rodney Stark
has put this in magnificent perspective:

> What was most remarkable about the Dark Ages was the way in which
> the full capacities of new technologies were rapidly recognized and
> widely adopted, as would be expected of a culture dominated by faith in
> progress.... Nor was innovation limited to technology; there was remark-
> able progress in areas of high culture—such as literature, art, and mu-
> sic—as well. Moreover, new technologies inspired new organizational
> and administrative forms, culminating in the birth of capitalism within
> the great monastic estates. This, in turn, prompted a complete theologi-
> cal reappraisal of the moral implications of commerce—the leading the-
> ologians rejected prior doctrinal objections to profits and interest,
> thereby legitimating the primary elements of capitalism. For all that these
> developments were of immense historical importance, they were in many
> respects a "secret revolution," as R. W. Southern so aptly put it—secret in
> the sense that we don't know who discovered what or, in most instances,
> even where or exactly when most of these innovations were accom-
> plished. What we do know is that they soon vaulted the West ahead of
> the rest of the world.[73]

Stark has done such a fine job capturing this phenomenon that it will

---

[73] *The Victory of Reason*, p. 37.

suffice to list in order the accomplishments he highlights.[74]

In terms of technological progress, power was harnessed by water mills and dams, which was previously provided by the abundance of slaves. The original use was the grinding of grain into flour, but later, with the advancement of gear assemblies, waterpower was used for cutting wood and stones, metalworking, and papermaking. Wind power was likewise harnessed, used primarily to drain swampland for agriculture. Horsepower came to find new uses as well, with the development of the horse collar – which for the first time enabled the horse to breath while pulling a load (!) – and horseshoes. This greatly increased the horse's utility, and so new plowing technology was developed to take advantage of this, which allowed for deep furrowing. The result was greatly increased productivity to support the burgeoning growth of towns and cities.

Fish farming likewise became an important activity, although by the 12th century it would be rendered superfluous by oceangoing fishing fleets – themselves an innovation of this civilization, as we will see below. Crop rotation schemes were devised using a three-field system, whereby field fertility was replenished by the planting of legumes and by lying fallow; the latter was needed only one-third of the time rather than half the time, as required by the Roman two-field practice.

Clothmaking also received a boost. "Until medieval Europeans invented treadle-powered looms, water-powered fulling machines, spinning wheels, and metal-toothed carding machines, cloth making was extremely labor intensive and was done on a very small scale, entirely by hand. Only the mechanization of cloth making allowed the growth of major cloth-making centers and industries, and these served as a major engine of commerce and, therefore, of finance" (p. 43). Other innovations included chimneys, eyeglasses, and clocks: "Sometime during the thirteenth century, someone somewhere in Europe invented a dependable mechanical clock. Soon, Europe was the only society where people really knew what time it was" (p. 44).

Medieval civilization likewise revolutionized warfare. Along with the horse collar and the horseshoe, stirrups and saddles with high pommels and cantles were introduced, enabling the appearance of the heavy ar-

---

[74] *The Victory of Reason,* pp. 37ff.

mored cavalry which wreaked such havoc among the traditional light cavalry of the Moors at the battle of Tours in 732 A. D., and would do so repeatedly during the Crusades. Similarly, gunpowder was first put to practical use in the 14th century, in the West – the rest is history – whereas the Chinese, who invented it, never took that fateful step.

Sea power was transformed by the introduction of the sternpost rudder, which replaced the steering oars previously in use. In addition, pulley constructions were introduced enabling a single helmsman to steer a large vessel. Innovations in shipbuilding drastically reduced the cost. And the cannon was introduced, making it possible to engage ships at a distance rather than having to ram them and/or engage in close-quarter hand-to-hand combat. But the most important innovation was the round ship, "a tall vessel with castles both fore and aft, multiple masts, and a complex set of sails, some of them square, some of them lateen (triangular)" (p. 47). These ships could carry much more gunnery and were capable of sailing the open seas as opposed to hugging the coast or remaining in closed seas like the Mediterranean. They could even sail in winter. To facilitate oceangoing sailing, the compass was put to use. Invented by both the Chinese and the Europeans, it was the latter who provided it with a compass card and sight, enabling sailors to determine headings. Charts showing compass headings enabled men to sail even in overcast conditions when the stars could not be consulted.

Now then:

> All of these remarkable developments can be traced to the unique Christian conviction that progress was a God-given obligation, entailed in the gift of reason. That new technologies and techniques would always be forthcoming was a fundamental article of Christian faith. Hence, no bishops or theologians denounced clocks or sailing ships—although both were condemned on religious grounds in various non-Western societies. Rather, many major technical innovations probably were made by monks and were eagerly adopted by the great monastic estates. Innovations spread very rapidly from one place to another because, contrary to the Dark Age tales concerning an insular and immobile Europe, the means of medieval transportation soon surpassed those of Roman times (p. 48).

Further innovations came in heavy transport (mainly thanks to the horse collar), in music (the invention of polyphony and musical notation), architecture (Gothic), literature (the formation of vernacular languages), education (universities), science (preparing the way for the "Copernican Revolution"), and capitalism, including double-entry bookkeeping and business lending at interest.

The Instrument of Stewardship: Law[75]

In all of these areas Christian civilization developed new and unprecedented ways to exercise the dominion mandate roundabout the temple service. But perhaps the most important was in the area of law and polity. Here as well, the role of the church was determinative.

The Transformation of the Polity

Kingship, the dominant form of polity, started out assuming a sacral character. The Holy Roman Emperor maintained this sacral typology more so than any other. He exercised priestly powers and constituted in himself the bond between heaven and earth. He also was the sovereign, the lawmaker and judge of all creatures. He himself was a king and a priest, claiming to be "after the order of Melchizedek," being the living representative of Christ on earth, and endowed with His authority.[76]

Armed with this self-conception, the Western emperors began to make connections with their counterparts in Byzantium to the east. This was a strategy pursued by the Ottos – Otto I (the Great, d. 973), Otto II (d. 983), and Otto III (d. 1002) – in order to furnish their claims to universal dominion with imperial substance. Otto II married the Byzantine princess Theophano, who then oversaw the education of Otto III; through this linkage, Byzantine imperial-court customs and culture were

---

[75] The discussion of law may be supplemented with these other works of mine: *A Common Law, Common Law & Natural Rights, The Debate that Changed the West,* and *Trojan Horse.* An excellent all-round survey is provided by Manlio Bellomo, *The Common Legal Past of Europe, 1000–1800.*

[76] See Kantorowicz's description: *The King's Two Bodies,* ch. III: "Christ-Centered Kingship."

imported into the Western imperial court, stamping its life and character. Byzantine emperor-centered ecclesiastical practice and liturgy also became established, as trappings of imperial authority, bolstering imperial claims to absolute authority in both spiritual and temporal matters. Perhaps most significant in this connection, at this time the Emperors began to draw upon Byzantine law, and in particular the law books of Justinian, to establish the source and the scope of imperial authority.[77]

But then along came Pope Gregory VII, who instigated the so-called "Papal Revolution" (otherwise known as the Investiture Crisis or the Gregorian Reform). Carried out between the years 1054 and 1122, the Papal Revolution constituted a revolutionary break with the received tradition precisely because it denied the Emperor's totalistic claims. The spiritual jurisdiction was separated out from the secular, creating the original "separation of powers."[78] The Emperor was denied his position as the vicar of Christ. He was stripped of divine status and liturgical focus; the church which he heretofore had headed was removed from his purview; the prel-

---

[77] "Hence it was from the late tenth century onwards that one witnessed the adoption of typical Byzantine emblems, rites, symbols, customs, nomenclatures, offices, and so on, which could be observed 'over there'. That therefore the very laws of the Roman emperors – that is, the law books of Justinian – were to become the laws of the Western emperors, is evident. The significant beginnings of this appropriation of the law books were already to be found in Otto III's reign, at the very end of the tenth century, and it would not be many decades before the full opulence of Justinian's *Code* was to be perceived in all its magnitude." Ullmann, *A History of Political Thought: The Middle Ages*, p. 97.
[78] "Many centuries later, the concept of the rule of law came to be identified with the separation of the legislative, administrative, and judicial powers. The later concept shared two features with the earlier concept. First, power was divided, although in the earlier period the 'checks and balances' had been provided chiefly by concurrent polities within the same territory rather than by concurrent branches of the same polity. Second, law was derived from, and rooted in, a reality that transcended the existing structure of political power. In the later period, that transcendent reality was found in human rights, democratic values, and other related beliefs. In the earlier period it had been found in divine and natural justice." Berman, *Law and Revolution,* p. 294.

ates which he was accustomed to put into office were taken out of his hands by the drastic measures of the Gregorian Reform. The Emperor henceforth was relegated to the status of temporal administrator of justice, the executor of laws pertaining to the affairs of secular life.

By asserting her jurisdiction over the realm of the sacred and, in so doing, opposing sacral empire, the church established the conditions through which the nations of Europe could develop independent existences in their own right. As medieval historian Joseph Strayer has noted, the Papal Revolution had several consequences favorable to the rise of territorial states:

1. The denial of imperial supremacy precipitated the recognition of territorial kings and princes as independent sovereigns. "Each kingdom or principality had to be treated as a separate entity; the foundations for a multi-state system had been laid."

2. The definition and promulgation of law codes based upon the distinction of the sacred and the secular, because the kings were considered administrators of secular justice. "The Gregorian reformers might believe that the Church defined what justice was, but even they admitted that in normal conditions it was the duty of secular rulers to see that justice was dispensed to the people.... But if they were to enforce justice, then codes of law must be developed and judicial institutions improved."

3. The strong emphasis on law meant that the developing European nations would become "law-states," whose reason for being would be found in maintaining an atmosphere of legal responsibility. "The state was based on law and existed to enforce law.... In no other political system was law so important; in no other society were lawyers to play such an important role."

4. More indirectly, the church also emphasized the importance of an educated "civil service" to carry out policies; university education, standard for clerics, became important also for laymen, and secular government modelled itself on church hierarchy and organization.[79]

The church pioneered the development of a new law-order which encompassed the entirety of Western Christendom. The growth of internal constitutions within the various nations, of bodies of rights and liberties,

---

[79] Strayer, *On the Medieval Origins of the Modern State*, pp. 22ff.

was mediated by the church. Legal science was fostered, necessary to the development of a system of law capable of meeting the challenge of the new situation. In this new legal science the main text used was the *Corpus Juris Civilis* of the Roman emperor Justinian, of which the Digest, or compilation of Roman lawyers' legal opinions, was the basic text for study in the developing curriculum.

But the nature of the influence of the Justinian law books must not be misunderstood. The *Corpus* was used as a guide for systematizing, for categorizing, and for orientation in the contemporary legal situation; but its content was not simply taken over and applied. "What was important about the study of Roman law was that it furnished a set of categories into which new ideas could be fitted and a vocabulary by which they could be described."[80] It was the canon law which, Berman claims, was the model law code for the West: "the first modern western legal system."[81]

The history of the way in which the Roman law of Justinian has been interpreted in the West is a crucially important one. In fact, by taking note of how the Roman law was being interpreted at any particular time, one can determine what kind of constitutional and political regime was being promoted, whether more or less constitutional, more or less absolutist. The kind of interpretation given to the Roman law is a touchstone for tracing the course of constitutional development.

During and immediately after the Papal Revolution the Justinian law was interpreted by the imperial party in as strictly a literal sense as possible, because such an interpretation lent strong support to the imperial claims of absolute authority. However, the yawning gap which existed between the kind of society envisaged in Justinian's law and that of contemporary feudal Europe was too great for such an effort to make very much headway. The Roman law was subjected to an intense effort of reinterpretation by various schools: the so-called "glossators" (so named because

---

[80] Strayer, *Medieval Origins*, p. 25.

[81] As the subtitle of ch. 5 proclaims: *Law and Revolution*, p. 199. For the relative influence of Roman law in the development of medieval legal science, see particularly pp. 120ff. and 204f. Berman's treatment does tend to underplay the importance of Roman law. See my *A Common Law* and Bellomo, *The Common Legal Past of Europe* for supplementary treatments of this theme.

they "glossed" or attached a running commentary to the given Roman law), the canon lawyers of the Papal party, and, a bit later on, the "post-Glossators" or Bartolists, beginning with the famed fourteenth-century jurist Bartolus of Saxoferrato, who reinterpreted the law in the light of republican liberties as were possessed and defended by the prospering Italian cities.[82]

The upshot of this effort at reinterpretation was to create a Roman law which stood at loggerheads with the original version. And this reinterpretation was embodied within a larger developing system of law and constitutional order expressing, and giving substance and stability to, the new reality of a European community of nations, itself forged through the cooperation of Papacy and territorial state over against Empire.

Jurisdiction and Sovereignty

Take for example the reinterpretation of the Roman law concepts of *imperium* and *jurisdictio*. In the original conception, *jurisdictio* referred to the authority of a judge to render judgment; *imperium,* to the basis for that authority, which lay in the Emperor. Thus, *jurisdictio* was a creature of *imperium* and wholly dependent upon *imperium* as the basis for its own authority. *Imperium,* in turn, was held solely by the Emperor. He might delegate *imperium* to lesser magistrates, but their *imperium* was entirely dependent upon his. As a result, all exercise of legitimate authority in society was derived from the Emperor, and entirely dependent upon him for its justification.

One of the great Roman lawyers of the Middle Ages, Azo (1150–1230), reversed this understanding of authority. Helped by the fact that nowhere in Justinian's texts were these concepts of *imperium* and *jurisdictio* explicitly spelled out, Azo proceeded to classify them in a manner exactly opposite to that described above. He made *imperium* a species of *jurisdictio;* furthermore, he interpreted *jurisdictio* to be held by lesser magistrates as well as the supreme magistrate (although acknowledging the Emperor to be the supreme magistrate), and that each level of *juris-*

---

[82] Skinner gives an excellent summary of the Bartolist project: Quentin Skinner, *The Foundations of Modern Political Thought: Volume One: The Renaissance*, pp. 9ff.

dictio was independent of the level above it, in the sense that it possessed a legitimacy in its own right. "Involved in Azo's analysis is a recognition that the jurisdiction and dominion – the sovereignty, as a later generation would say – of kings, princes, heads of municipal governments, and other magistrates are not derived from the jurisdiction and dominion of the emperor."[83]

Thus Azo provided a definition of political sovereignty expressive of the new realities of post-Papal Revolution Europe, capturing in this conception the decentralization of political authority characteristic of the medieval constitution.

This is how the tradition of limited sovereignty became established. But there is another form of sovereignty, known as absolute. Between these two there has been a struggle, and much of the history of Western civilization is stamped by that struggle.[84] Basically, absolute sovereignty holds that the state is the source of law (the primacy of legislation), while limited sovereignty holds that the state only recognizes and confirms law which develops through the interaction of social actors (the primacy of custom), and that this confirmation occurs under the leading of a higher law (the law of God). Absolute sovereignty makes the state a law unto itself, while limited sovereignty restricts the jurisdiction of the state and makes it amenable to correction from outside.

Public and Private Law

A crucial area of difference between these two forms of sovereignty is found with regard to ownership. In the case of limited sovereignty, sovereignty is in the service of property, while in the case of absolute sovereignty, the relationship is reversed: property is in the service of sovereignty. This is a crucial distinction to make, if one is to understand stewardship aright.

Because limited sovereignty serves private ownership, public law serves private law.[85]

---

[83]Berman, *Law and Revolution,* pp. 289–292; quote on p. 291.

[84] See *A Common Law* for an outline of that history.

[85] As McIlwain pointed out, this was a major distinguishing characteristic of Ro-

The public-law/private-law distinction is prior to all legal philoso-phizing; it has to be assumed – it cannot be ignored. Even the socialist legal philosopher Gustav Radbruch recognized this. "The concepts 'pri-vate' and 'public law' are not concepts of positive law that could just as well be eliminated from a particular positive law order, but much rather logically precede the practical application of law and seek application ahead of time in any practical application of law. They are a priori law concepts.... The distinction between private and public law is anchored in the concept of law itself."[86] Radbruch argues that the priority one gives to private over public law or vice versa is historically determined and as such is more or less a matter of preference; but in terms of limited sover-eignty the priority must go to private law.

We say that public law exists to serve private law. This restricts public law to the regulation of civil government. It ensures that civil government is able to function properly. But it does not tell us for what greater goal civil government functions. It does not provide the rationale of civil gov-ernment; it only delineates an internal structure. The end of civil govern-ment extends beyond public law to all the associations of which society is comprised. And the law which it maintains to regulate the interrela-tions of these associations, the law regulating and coordinating their sev-eral activities, is private law. As such, private law functions as an integrat-ing common law.

What enables private law to perform this function is its unique struc-ture, which cannot be subsumed into public law. Private law has its own independent existence. This is the burden of Ernest J. Weinrib's im-portant book, *The Idea of Private Law*.[87] Private law, Weinrib argues, is

---

man law. As he writes in his *Constitutionalism: Ancient and Modern*, "undoubt-edly one of [the Romans'] greatest permanent contributions to constitutional-ism was the distinction they made, more clearly than it had been made before, or was to be made for long afterward, between the *jus publicum* [public law] and the *jus privatum* [private law]—a distinction that lies to this day behind the whole history of our legal safeguards of the rights of the individual against en-croachment of government" (p. 46).

[86] *Rechtsphilosophie* [Philosophy of Law], pp. 220–221.

[87] Cambridge, MA: Harvard University Press, 1995.

characterized by the bilateral relationship of the parties involved. Two parties, joined by an action, one party acting, one party being acted upon. What flows out of such an action, whether agreeable or disagreeable, forms the subject matter of private law. Concepts of distribution and administration do not enter into this equation, because such concepts import considerations that do not flow from the relation. The resolution is inherent in the relation, and depends upon the consideration of the action itself.

The private-law relationship is necessary because it is the expression of free and independent actors. For society is something other than community. In fact, society is composed of communities. As Johannes Althusius wrote in his *Politica Methodice Digesta,* society is a complex of associations beginning with the family and progressing to the state. Individuals exercise the right of ownership primarily through these associations. (As such, the charge lodged against private ownership, that it is a system of possessive individualism and thus antisocial, is from the start categorically refuted.) Private ownership is ownership by private associations, beginning with the family. Purely individual ownership forms the exception, not the rule. And it is the interactions *between* owners, thus between these, shall we say, ownership entities, that form the subject matter of private law.

The two kinds of justice first delineated by Aristotle, distributive justice and commutative justice, highlight this difference. Distributive justice involves the proper distribution *within* a given organization or community. It refers to goods common to all, owned by all, to be distributed by a central authority, in terms of what each member merits. Commutative justice, on the other hand, refers to exchange *between* organizations or communities, regarding goods not shared or owned in common but rather owned severally by the exchanging parties and therefore not falling under the authority of a distributing agent, but free to be disposed of by the transacting parties. Thus, the difference between commutative and distributive justice is based on the question of ownership. Within the bounds of ownership, distributive justice prevails; outside the bounds of ownership, thus *between* owners, among free, "autonomous" actors, commutative justice does. It is the difference in ownership which explains the difference in law.

Private law gives expression to commutative justice. It applies to relations between these owners; as we said, it is an external, coordinating law. Internally, ownership entities are governed by law-orders peculiar to each – family law, corporate law, laws governing foundations, clubs, etc.[88] These law-orders, being internal, are expressive of the principles of distributive justice. Private law does not extend into the internal affairs of these associations, forming as they do a world of their own.

Public law, we said, concerns the internal functioning of the public association, hence civil government. It is therefore concerned with those things the citizens hold in common. Common property is part of this, but mainly it has to do with government functions, something which all citizens share in, either in administering those functions (public office) or paying for them (taxation). For example, voting rights fall under public law. Constitutional law, fiscal law, administrative law, all fall under the category of public law. All these forms of law, being internal to the functioning of government, are likewise covered by the principles of distributive justice. Understood in this manner, public law is the *internal* law (*lex proprium*) of the association known as the state.

With these understandings we are now in a position to situate stewardship within the societal framework. Stewardship concerns the administration of affairs *within* any of the various associations and organizations making up society. The largest of these, of course, is the state, and as we have seen, the state includes within its purview the common or public property which is the possession of all the citizens together. Yet even this category cannot be extended to cover private property, neither can the state use its regulatory powers to surreptitiously undermine the regime of private property. Both of these behaviors undermine pluralist associationalism. Neither answers to the doctrine of stewardship. In fact, they contradict it.[89] *Public law is not common law.*

---

[88] Althusius referred to these laws as *leges propriae,* "proper laws," to be distinguished from the *jus* or *lex commune,* "common law." Every form of association has one. "They differ in each specie of association according as the nature of each requires." *Politica Methodice Digesta,* I. §19, in Alvarado, *The Debate that Changed the West,* p. 96.

[89] See my *A Theology of Nature,* pp. 27ff.

The War on Private Law

Contemporary legal science, in thrall to absolute sovereignty, seeks to turn this relation on its head; it seeks to make public law common law. As such, over the past 200 years a war has been conducted against private law. Private law is a "bourgeois capitalist" concept that has no standing in a truly social order.

If the 19th century was the century in which the theory of the attack on private law was developed, the 20th century was the century in which this attack was actually launched. The subsumption of private by public law has been the chief focus of socialist regimes. Radbruch viewed it this way: "for an individualistic legal order, public law – the state – is only the restrictive protective framework revolving around private law and private property; for a social legal order the reverse is true – the private law is only a provisionally preserved and ever-shrinking space for private initiative within the all-encompassing public law."[90] The agenda is clear: private law as an independent structure has no legitimate standing in the socialist system.

But private law, being expressive of commutative justice, has its own inner logic, its own structure which must be respected in lawmaking of any shape. Currently, legislation is the primary source of law, both public and private. The problem with this is that legislation is primarily directed by considerations of distributive and not commutative justice. This is because the legislature is oriented towards public law, it historically has been shaped by public law, and it sees its mission in terms of public law.[91] Add to this the modern social-democratic bias in favor of public law as in all-encompassing "social" law, and one begins to see the danger of modern legislation to the regime of private law.

This underlying bias viewing distributive justice and by extension public law as a kind of remedy against the "individualism" of private law has a long history. Hugo Grotius was the first to pit commutative justice against distributive justice, but he did so in favor of commutative justice.[92]

---

[90] "Vom individualistischen zum sozialen Recht" [From Individualistic Law to Social Law]" (1930), p. 40.

[91] See Hayek, *Law, Legislation and Liberty* for a comprehensive exposition.

[92] *A Common Law*, pp. 92ff. See also *The Debate that Changed the West*.

He created the prototypical classical liberal legal framework, whereby commutative justice is strict justice, and thus capable of being expressed in civil law, while distributive justice, which he described as a moral rather than a strictly juridical category, is unamenable to expression in law.

Later in the same century, Gottfried Wilhelm Leibniz turned this construction on its head, arguing that commutative justice formed a lower sort of justice that needed to be adjusted and corrected by distributive justice, which served as a principal of equity, correcting undesirable results arising from the administration of this lower form of justice.

G. W. F. Hegel took Leibniz's principle further, arguing that civil society – the private-law society – needed the corrective and leading role of the state to rectify its inevitable "conflicts of interest." The entire structure of social democracy and the welfare state is built on this concept.

This is the unexamined presupposition underlying the typical modern concept of justice and law. Private law is supposed to foster conflicts of interest and unjust outcomes. This is an expression of the conflict-of-interest worldview that I discussed in my book *A Common Law* (pp. 106ff.). The question is, are conflicts of interest spawned by the regime of private law? Do private associations in their mutual interactions require the guidance and distributing power of an overarching state? Or is there a built-in structure of harmonization via commutation that enables the regime of private law to function quite well on its own, making intervention superfluous if not downright destructive?

This requires a closer look. There are a variety of terms that express the principle underlying private law, including commutation, restitution, reciprocity. These in turn are based in the prototypical *lex talionis* ("an eye for an eye") of Leviticus 24. It is indeed an ancient principle of justice and one that in itself no one has ever presumed to find fault with, at least in principle, although the literal application of the *lex talionis* is adhered to only in primitive cultures – more advanced ones substitute a penalty considered equal, though not literally so (for example, one is not literally required to give up an eye if one causes blindness in someone else). Problems arise only upon consideration of outcomes. For private law is no respecter of persons. It does not take into consideration the relative conditions of the parties involved; it only takes cognizance of the matter involving them. Thus, for example, if a poor person steals from a rich one, private law requires restitution regardless of the fact that one has much and one has little. Private law only sees that one has robbed another, creating a disturbance in the legal order that must be restored.

If this was all there was to public concern, then the criticism of a lack of "social concern" would have some validity. And with classical liberalism this was indeed the case. The restriction of the role of the state to "strict," i.e., commutative justice combined with the elimination of any public role for the church left a void that could only be filled by social action and the rise of the welfare state.

But this is where an understanding of the historical development of law in the West pays dividends. For once we understand the role the church played in this development, then we can see how it is that the regime of private law was enabled, indeed allowed, to develop. This could only take place because a balance was achieved whereby social concern indeed was taken into account in public policy.

This balance was achieved because two institutions were concerned with the public square, not just one. While the state was vested with the ministry of justice, the church was vested with the ministry of mercy. By virtue of this jurisdiction, the church exercised a diaconate by which poverty could be alleviated, even while the state maintained "strict" justice.

But along came the Enlightenment, and with it the banishment of the church from the public square. The absence of social concern gave birth to the "social question." Thus abandoned, private law became the scapegoat.

This has led to the anomaly whereby the modern ethicist may yield the point that the principle underlying private law is just, but then argues that its outworking is unjust. The argument used to justify this sleight of hand runs along the lines of "moral man, immoral society" or "structural sin." We get "formal versus substantive justice" and "outcome-based ethics." The individuals involved have done nothing wrong, yet the outcome of their actions is deemed undesirable. Therefore something must be done to correct this unforeseen consequence. Therefore private law cannot be allowed an autonomous existence. Therefore economic freedom cannot be allowed free rein. It must be restricted for the sake of "social justice."

This is where distributive justice invades the proper sphere of commutative justice. Public law in the guise of social justice begins to subsume private law. It does so through legislation. Which is why the question of the source of law is so important. If legislation is the only legitimate source of law, then private law as an autonomous regime is imperiled. Because, as we have seen, legislation is inherently distributive. Its encroachment upon the sphere of private law is usually to bend outcomes away from how they would turn out in terms of the justice of the case.[93]

Private law must be defended from these encroachments. It must be recognized as an autonomous realm, indispensable for the functioning of a free society, a society of associations. It therefore must be allowed to grow and develop in terms of the interactions of these associations, in line with the principles of commutative justice. On this realization depend the freedoms we treasure.

And on this basis depends our pursuit of stewardship. Because stewardship, being a function of ownership, cannot function without private law.

The Theocratic Ordering of Life

That these things have not always been recognized as the living, historical realities that they are, as the actual as opposed to the imagined manner in which Western civilization has developed, stands to reason. The historiography – as opposed to the history – of the West has been scandalously usurped by interests having no interest in recognizing the central role of the church in the development of this civilization. I have only to mention the two primary versions of history currently held to – the Marxist (progressive liberal) and the Whig (classical liberal). These two rule the roost, dominate the mindset, and cannot escape the death spiral which they have helped to initiate. There is only one escape from

---

[93] For this reason Hayek spoke of the "mirage" of social justice. For to even speak of social justice, one must first eliminate the social, and convert everything into the communal, whereby society becomes one big community. A society of free and equal actors falls under a different regime of justice, viz. commutative. Social justice can only function within a community or organization – which is why those advocating social justice likewise work toward the elimination of several property. See Hayek, *The Mirage of Social Justice,* vol. 1 of *Law, Legislation and Liberty.*

their deadly embrace, and that is to recover the understanding of the cen-
trality of God's temple – the church – to civilization. And when that is
put into practice, it will redound to the salvation of nature as well.

The person who best understood the role of the church in civilization
was A. A. van Ruler (1908–1970). Van Ruler was a pastor in the Dutch
national church and a professor of theology at Utrecht University. He
was also a prolific writer and speaker, who among other things broadcast
a weekly meditation over national radio for more than 20 years, attracting
an average of 450,000 listeners.[94] This is quite a number, something like
4% of the total population at the time.

In his book *Religie en Politiek* [Religion and Politics], written during
World War II, Van Ruler laid down some fundamentals with regard to
the role of the church in society which are expressive of the biblical principles we have outlined in this book. He spoke of the church not simply
as a voice, proclaiming the Word of God and adopting a critical stance
vis-à-vis the surrounding world, but as an ordering power roundabout
Word and Sacrament.

First, roundabout the Word.

> The preaching of the church is not only concerned with an otherworldly
> salvation for immortal souls, so that the church with her preaching is
> there for those souls with a view to heaven, but ... it also concerns the
> ministry of the Word, wherein the questions of the day are set in the light
> of the truth which comes to us in revelation. Everything is discussed in
> the pulpit; everything from marriage, to family, to school, to work, to
> society, to the state, to science, to art. And then all of that, when the
> Word is ministered with regard to it, is not only set in the right light, but
> is all set right by it. The Word puts everything in its place. Things are what
> the Word says of them. Thus the Word orders life. This is not a matter of
> contemplation, but it is a reality that comes to pass. In this the church is
> faithful to the earth (p. 177).

---

[94] "Arnold van Ruler, de theoloog die zending weer op de kaart zette" [Arnold
van Ruler, who put missions on the map again]. *Nederlands Dagblad,* 13 De-
cember 2018. URL: https://www.nd.nl/geloof/geloof/539591/arnold-van-ru-
ler-de-theoloog-die-zending-weer-op-de-kaart-zette

Preaching is not just about eternal salvation in the beyond, it is about the here and now, because God's Word is about the here and now. It "puts everything in its place," it "orders life."

This ordering principle then extends to the sacraments, beginning with baptism:

> The church baptizes, but it baptizes children. And infant baptism gives the sacrament and thus the church an enormous extension in the plane of earthly life. It is not individuals lifted out of the mass of destruction into a supernatural territory; rather, the church enters into the national stock and associates itself with the popular stock and with national life (p. 177).

The sacrament of baptism rightly understood is not for a select group of individuals, but for families, and for the family writ large – the nation. "Go therefore and make disciples of all the nations, baptizing them in the name of the Father and the Son and the Holy Spirit" (Matthew 28: 19). In so reaching into earthly life, the church makes holy what was once profane. "For the unbelieving husband is sanctified through his wife, and the unbelieving wife is sanctified through her believing husband; for otherwise your children are unclean, but now they are holy" (1 Cor. 7: 14).

The sacrament of the Lord's Supper puts the finishing touch on this arrangement:

> And so it is with the Lord's Supper. The church celebrates the Lord's Supper, but roundabout the sacrament of the Lord's Supper she observes the *censura morum*, the discipline of morals, and enters in an ordering manner into national life. In this way the church creates cultures. In this too she is faithful to the earth (p. 177).

This *censura morum*, this "censure of morals," has a long history. Johannes Althusius wrote extensively about it in his *Political Methodice Digesta*, although the details of what he had to say about it reflect the mores of the times, specifically in the maintenance of sumptuary laws.[95] What

---

[95] For an abridged translation, see *The Debate that Changed the West*, pp. 169–171.

matters is the general equity. And the general equity of this task is that it sets the stage for the law as promulgated and maintained by the state – the law which we saw elaborated in the previous section. Van Ruler explains it like this:

> The church not only witnesses, she also orders life. To say that the church only testifies critically, only negatively, that she raises her voice only when things head the wrong way in the world, e.g., in the state, is clearly incorrect. In any case it must also be said that the church also forms, also positively testifies, that it is her right and her duty to indicate, not only how *not* to do it, but also how *to* do it. And even that is not enough. The church is not satisfied with talking. She also gets to work and herself takes up the ordering of life. Even today the church demands submission to her ordinances. And it is not at all wrong if the church in her *corpus juris* [body of law] takes up a piece of marriage law or also a piece of commercial or labor law. In principle, the church is busy with this every day. And on her terrain she finds the state, and in the civil magistrate she greets the servant of God, to whom this concrete order of life, with which she herself began roundabout Word and sacrament, is commended for further elaboration and application. Church and state are intertwined over the entire length and breadth of life. The task of the state can only be seen as an extension of the *censura-morum* task of the consistory. This ordering of life – let it be said again – is something that takes place. It does not proceed through individual belief. Confession is not the same as conviction, but is more than conviction, it is the echo of the mighty Word of God in existence. Man is sucked into it and consumed. Confession and sacrifice belong together (pp. 177–178).

This is what it means for the temple to be set in the center of the social order. This is what Zechariah meant when he wrote, "In that day there will be inscribed on the bells of the horses, 'HOLY TO THE LORD.' And the cooking pots in the LORD's house will be like the bowls before the altar. And every cooking pot in Jerusalem and in Judah will be holy to the LORD of hosts; and all who sacrifice will come and take of them and boil in them. And there will no longer be a Canaanite in the house of the LORD of hosts in that day" (14: 20–21). *Pace* Oliver Wendell Holmes, the life of the law is neither experience nor logic – it is "the holiness without which no one will see the Lord" (Hebrews 12: 14, NASB 2020).

That is what *biblical* stewardship looks like.

THE MODERN CONCEPT OF GLOBAL STEWARDSHIP

Given this understanding, it will become clear that the concept and agenda of global stewardship, stewardship of "the planet," stands four-square opposed to the stewardship espoused in the Bible, based as it is on private ownership roundabout the temple. Instead, the concept of global stewardship bases itself on the understanding outlined in the previous section, of distributive "social" justice "correcting" the failures of the private sector and indeed eliminating that sector in order to manage the natural world directly. It overthrows the associationalism of independent ownership entities in its drive to convert society into a single monolithic organization, one in which all relations are internal and directed from above. A centralized collectivism is the end, all else – race relations, gender "equity," sexual liberation, environmental protection, Christian "stewardship" – are means.

This is behind the massive expansion both of "public" ownership of land and of far-reaching intervention in the rights of private owners.[96] Both are expressions of an overlordship that presumes to preserve the land and the natural world from the depredations of conflict-ridden private ownership. In fact, the motivation is clearly the *primacy* of the natural world and the *subordination of humanity* to the natural world. For human interaction and intervention are evils, at best necessary ones. Of course, to accomplish this, an all-powerful regulating and directing agency is required.

All of this is supposed to be in the best interest both of humanity and the natural world. But it does beg the question – is this where we end up when we ask, "What Would Jesus Do?" Where is God in all of this?

That the Christian wing of the environmentalist movement does not seem overly keen to take notice of that question, is something to take notice of. An example is the progression shown in the popular *Earthkeeping* books issued under the auspices of Calvin College and published by Eerdmans. The first edition, published in 1980, was subtitled "Christian Stew-

---

[96] See *A Theology of Nature,* pp. 27ff.

ardship of Natural Resources." The second, published in 1991, was subtitled "Stewardship of Creation." What motivated the change? First, regarding "natural resources": "To the Christian the earth ought to be neither 'Nature' (which suggests its elevation to divinity) nor 'resources' (which implies its degradation to a mere stockpile of raw material awaiting the action of human industry). Nor is it simply the abstract 'environment.' It is rather 'creation,' a word which reminds us not only of the Creator, but also of our status as creatures and our task as stewards" (p. x). So *nature* "suggests an elevation to divinity" and *environment* is too abstract? Methinks one has become overly fastidious here, in particular in view of the fact that Christian environmentalists are always making use of these very words without subjecting themselves to the least criticism. And *resources* – really? The word is too instrumental? Is this not a sign that our Christian environmentalists are no longer interested in any subordination of nature to the needs of man? So much for the dominion mandate.

And then there is the rationale for the elimination of the word *Christian:* "We also have dropped 'Christian' from the subtitle, for it gave the impression that the sorts of actions we were proposing were incumbent only on Christians. The stewardship we are recommending is not only a Christian task, but belongs to all human creatures. We believe more than ever that only through the new life in Christ — the renewal of creation that begins with the renewing of the Creator's failed, flawed, willful stewards — will that stewardship of creation which more and more people are seeking to exercise ever be possible. But it is not only to Christians that the book is addressed. Rather, it is addressed to all stewards of creation" (p. x). Here we have a *contradictio in terminis in optima forma.* Either the salvation wrought by Christ *is* required for the renewal of the creation – in which case mere human action is useless and conversion of the nations is required – or mere human action contributes to, and even brings about, the renewal of creation, in which case the salvation wrought by Christ is *not* required to bring this about. But fence-straddling is *de rigueur* among our Christian environmentalists.

This is remindful of a previous episode in the history of the church, when the doctrines of socialism had become fashionable and were displacing orthodoxy in the churches. Many churchmen and -women had become enamored of this new doctrine and were finding it difficult to maintain both their faith and their newfound commitment. Writing in 1909, Mauro highlighted this:

> Many earnest persons who are to-day advocating more or less of the industrial principles of Socialism are at the same time holding on (nominally at least) to the main doctrines of Christianity. But it will be readily seen that these persons as *Christians* are apathetic, while as *Socialists* they are full of propagating zeal. The converts they make are converts to Socialism, not to Christ; and the places of these propagandists, when vacant, will be acceptably filled, and all they are now doing will be just as well done, by others who make no profession at all of Christianity. It is quite compatible with much of what is taught in the churches to-day to do homage to Man himself as his own deliverer.[97]

So we begin to realize that for the new Christianity it is not the church which is central and humanity which needs to recognize that, but quite the reverse: stewardship-oriented humanity is central and the church needs to recognize that; Christians are only a part of the whole, a subset of the group "stewards." Which begs the question: is it the calling of Christians and of the church (=part) to be subsumed into the world (=whole), without any recognition of their status as New Temple and New Creation[98]?

So much is certain: we now know who the "us" is to whom World Vision was referring in its statement on environmental action (see p. 34 above). It is *indiscriminate humanity.*

What we are facing here is nothing less than absorption into a brotherhood-of-man universalist religion. Mauro provides a trenchant analysis and critique of this.[99] The socialist framework has since been expanded into the areas of race, gender, and the environment, to name a few. Even so, the basic characteristics remain.

"The faith of the world is based on Man, the fundamental principle of

---

[97] *The Number of Man: The Climax of Civilization,* pp. 69–70.

[98] Dumbrell, *The End of the Beginning,* chs. "The New Temple" and "The New Creation."

[99] *The Number of Man: The Climax of Civilization,* pp. 55ff.

that faith being that Man possesses the inherent power to lift himself out of all evil conditions, and to overcome all existing hindrances to his progress" (pp. 65–66). This faith is on display throughout the Christian writings on "earthkeeping." Christianity is not considered to be *the* solution to a fallen world; instead, Christians (which is something else) are to *contribute* to a solution. But Mauro makes the obvious point: "a fundamental proposition of Christian doctrine is that man is impotent and untrustworthy. 'Put not your trust in princes' (Ps. cxlvi. 3). 'Cursed be the man that trusteth in man, and maketh flesh his arm' (Jer. xvii. 5). It is impossible to conceive of a religious system more opposed to Christianity than one whose main teaching is that man may and must put his trust in his own inherent power and goodness" (p. 66). Do our Christian environmentalists suppose that mere cooperation with the world will accomplish God's purposes?

Alas Babylon

We have run headlong into a condition which is increasingly self-consciously God-forsaking. Humankind has decided to solve its problems in its own strength, on its own terms. What does this sound like? A reprise of the tower of Babel? Who could possibly disagree? Mauro elucidates:

> Hence the idea that stands out prominently upon the surface of the thought of to-day is *confidence in Man*. This is not individual self-confidence, which is quite a different thing. It is a *collective* self-confidence. The masses are being diligently schooled by a variety of teachers, and for widely varying purposes, to think of Humanity as an entity. In discussing questions of the hour, much is made of the interests, prospects, welfare, and progress of "Society" rather than of individuals, of mankind rather than of men and women.... People are looking to Man himself, to his own achievements, his ingenuity and inventive abilities, his industry and daring, and whatever other powers he is supposed to possess, whether developed or undeveloped, for the accomplishment of all the good that is in view for collective humanity (pp. 66–67).

What stands in the way of this? The teaching of Christianity, which states that there is no united humanity but rather a great divide in humanity which can only be eliminated by a final separation. As Mauro notes, "The propagation of the idea of the 'Solidarity of Man,' or the essential identity of the interests of all mankind... tends to obliterate the important teaching of Scripture that instead of one united humanity having a common destiny, there are two great sections of humanity, one composed of those who have life through faith in the Son of God, and the other of those who have not life;– one embracing the children of God and the other the children of wrath" (p. 68).

This is not simply eschatological. It runs right through the relations, the policies, the destinies of the nations in the here and now. And the outward shape it is taking is the elimination of differences, those things which stand in the way of unification. One of those is national sovereignty, that relic of God's merciful judgment on the original tower of Babel. That stumbling block must be removed in favor of transnational government. Another, of course, is the church, with her message of salvation in Christ alone. "For we are a fragrance of Christ to God among those who are being saved and among those who are perishing; to the one an aroma from death to death, to the other an aroma from life to life. And who is adequate for these things?" (2 Cor. 2: 15–16). The church stands in the way of unification; therefore, measures must be taken if a unification of humanity is to be attained.

> The idea of a consolidated humanity is a brilliant and fascinating conception. It captures the imagination, and is capable of arousing the enthusiasm necessary to insure success. To what more worthy end could man devote his wonderful powers and faculties than to the banishment of all poverty, cruelty, selfishness, warfare, and other ills that bring miseries upon humanity? And all this, and more, may be accomplished through the unification of human society, the welding of all human units into one great brotherhood, wherein the rights of all individuals will be equally sacred and equally the concern of the whole system (Mauro, p. 71).

"And the Lord said, "Behold, they are one people, and they all have the same language. And this is what they began to do, and now nothing which they purpose to do will be impossible for them" (Gen. 11: 6).

This captivating ideal involves not merely industrial unification, but also the harmonization of all religious views. Indeed, a universal religion is an absolute necessity if the ideal is ever to be realized; for nothing has given rise to more hatred, antagonism, and bloodshed, than conflicting religious views. Religious antagonisms *must be* totally eliminated. Hence the strong appeals and efforts that are being made for the cessation of religious strife, as well as of industrial strife. The great thought which is throbbing at this moment in the heart of humanity is nothing less than the reversal of what took place at Babel, when the Lord confounded their language and scattered them abroad from thence upon the face of all the earth. And when this proposed consolidation of humanity has been accomplished, the re-united elements of human society will be free to resume the building of the tower whose top was to reach unto heaven (Mauro, pp. 71–72).

Is this what Christians are called to do? Efface the difference; follow Voltaire's advice and *écrasez l'infâme?* May it never be!

For we are the temple of the living God; just as God said,
"I will dwell in them and walk among them;
and I will be their God, and they shall be my people.
Therefore, come out from their midst and be separate," says the Lord.
"and do not touch what is unclean;
and I will welcome you.
And I will be a father to you,
and you shall be sons and daughters to me,"
says the Lord Almighty (2 Cor. 6: 16–18).

For then and only then "the creation itself also will be set free from its slavery to corruption into the freedom of the glory of the children of God" (Rom. 8: 21).

"He who testifies to these things says, 'Yes, I am coming quickly.' Amen. Come, Lord Jesus" (Rev. 22: 20).

CONCLUSION

Does God care for oxen? Yes, He does. But that does not mean that He puts them, or any other creature, on the same level as human beings. As we have seen, Paul is explicit: "Or is He speaking altogether for our sake? Yes, for our sake it was written, because the plowman ought to plow in hope, and the thresher to thresh in hope of sharing the crops" (1 Cor. 9: 10). God is speaking *altogether* [pantós] for our sake, which means entirely, completely. In other words, the ox is nothing unless it is brought in relation to man. By extension, then, nature itself is nothing unless it is brought in relation to man. God uses nature in His training of man, His disciplining of man, His punishment of man, as is so richly illustrated in passages like Deuteronomy 8 (see p. 54 above). Nature's goodness, beauty, bounty, on the one hand, and malevolence and fearfulness on the other, are instruments in God's hand to discipline His children and bring about His kingdom. Reward and punishment – this is the purpose of nature as revealed in Scripture.

To paraphrase Jesus (Mark 2: 27):

NATURE WAS MADE FOR MAN, AND NOT MAN FOR NATURE

So then, stewardship cannot be nature-centric. It cannot be that man is to serve nature. That is an inversion of the God-given order. It is a violation of the second of the Ten Commandments (see p. 44 above). We are not to serve these graven images – for that is what they are – of the natural world. We are not to bow down before these imaginary romanticized constructs erected to fill the place of the worship of the One True God. And we must cease and desist from spreading this false teaching in churches, in pulpits, in Bible study groups, wherever doctrine is discussed. "We are no longer to be children, tossed here and there by waves, and carried about by every wind of doctrine, by the trickery of men, by craftiness in deceitful scheming." It is time we put an end to this, precisely in order to build the temple by which alone the presence of God, and so

Paradise, can be restored.[100] How do we do that? By "speaking the truth in love," says Paul. Speaking the *truth* in love. Love does not contradict truth! By so doing, "we are to grow up in all aspects into Him, who is the head, even Christ, from whom the whole body, being fitted and held together by that which every joint supplies, according to the proper working of each individual part, causes the growth of the body for the building up of itself in love" (Eph. 4: 14–16). So will this body grow, this temple out of which true blessing will flow even unto the natural world. For false teaching does no one any favors, least of all nature.

There can therefore be no such thing as stewardship of nature writ large except in the most analogous, even allegorical sense. At least, if we are to take the Bible seriously instead of hitching it to imaginary ideological wagons. Concretely, there is stewardship of this or that piece of property, stewardship of this or that specific group, association, or organization; there is no stewardship whereby ownership, and that which ownership entails, is short-circuited through the explicit or implicit exercise of a presumed eminent domain by the state.[101] Property owners are stewards under God, responsible to Him for the use they put to that property. "I am the LORD, that is My name; I will not give My glory to another" (Isaiah 42: 8) – not even to the state. That is the biblical doctrine of stewardship.

And so we come to the end of our excursion into the meaning of this doctrine. Just one concluding remark: The basic problem confronting the Christian environmentalist is that he or she champions a stewardship which is no stewardship at all, it having in the nature of the case *Ni Dieu ni maître* [neither God nor master]. This is because the secularist, with whom cooperation is so fervently sought, acknowledges none. As such, "stewardship" exercised by all of mankind is an empty phrase. The upshot is mastery, not stewardship – a mastery in which some particular sliver of mankind exercises hegemony over the rest, all in the name of planetary salvation. Is this the stewardship that answers to Scripture? We think not.

---

[100] David Chilton, *Paradise Restored.*

[101] For more on this, see *A Theology of Nature*, pp. 24–29.

APPENDIX: ENVIRONMENTALISM AND CHRISTIANITY'S ETHIC OF DOMINION

First published in The Journal of Christian Reconstruction, *Vol. XI, No. 2, 1986–87, pp. 201–215.*

This was my first ever published article. I wrote it soon after returning from service in the Peace Corps as an extension forester in Paraguay. At the time, I had decided against the further pursuit of a career in forestry. As such, this article constituted a bridge from my hitherto contemplated career (in fact, I had been accepted to Yale University's forestry school to complete a master's degree in international forestry) to a career in researching, writing, translating, and ultimately publishing. Admittedly, being a product of youthful exuberance, it is less nuanced than my later work. And it contains a few positions which I have since revised. I will take notice of these by interspersing comments between square brackets. But the continuity of thought over a career spanning some 40 years as of this writing speaks for itself.

In the May, 1981 edition of *Audubon* magazine, Ron Wolf presented his view of then Secretary of the Interior James Watt's resources management philosophy, in behalf of the environmentalist movement. Watt at the time was redirecting the Department towards a management strategy of development as opposed to preservation, in line with the Reagan administration's sympathy for the condition of the "Sagebrush Rebels" in the West. Those people saw government lands as the key to their continued well-being, and were understandably opposed to environmentalist efforts to withdraw from development vast amounts of acreage. Environmentalists, in turn, saw Watt as a "fox in the chicken coop," giving up for despoliation lands which he was sworn to protect.

Wolf's article was entitled "God, James Watt, and the Public's Land." He saw, underneath the squabble over land use, a war of religion taking place: two religions fighting for philosophical control of "the public's land." Environmentalism, he wrote, was characterized by a sense of identification with nature. "In general this broad tradition has given rise to forms of belief in which a person's spiritual, physical, and even economic well-being are considered to derive from his rapport with all of creation, from being in tune with the infinite." He contrasts this view with that of Watt's fundamentalist Christianity, of man's dominion over nature as ordained by God. Wolf says it is this attitude of dominion that is the cause of environmental despoliation. This is the root of the prob- [202] lem, he writes, and the real point of battle between Watt and environmentalism.

The thesis that orthodox Christianity is the cause of ecological disruption by our society is not new with Wolf. Aldo Leopold, whose book *A Sand County Almanac* (1949) has been termed "one of the bibles" of environmentalism,[102] advanced this idea in his critique of utilitarian conservation philosophy. He wrote, "Conservation is getting nowhere because it is incompatible with our Abrahamic concept of land. We abuse land because we regard it as a commodity belonging to us."[103] And again: "In human history, we have learned (I hope) that the conqueror role is eventually self-defeating ... In the biotic community, a parallel situation exists. Abraham knew exactly what the land was for: it was to drip milk and honey into Abraham's mouth. At the present moment, the assurance with which we regard this assumption is inverse to the degree of our education."[104] This hostility towards the ethic of dominion was made orthodoxy with Prof. Lynn White Jr.'s article "The Historical Roots of Our Ecologic Crisis" (first published in *Science,* 10 March 1967, and reprinted many times thereafter). After describing the impetus which Western Christianity gave to the development of science and technology, White decries the impact of these developments on the environment, attributing their abuse to the world-view which contributed so much to their appearance. He writes that "somewhere over a century ago science and technology—hitherto quite separate activities—joined to give mankind powers which, to judge by many of the ecologic efforts, are out of control. If so,

[102] William Tucker, *Progress and Privilege: America in the Age of Environmentalism* (Garden City, New York: Anchor Press/Doubleday, 1982), p. 130.

[103] Aldo Leopold, *A Sand County Almanac* (New York: Oxford Univ. Press, 1966 [1949]), x.

[104] *Ibid.,* p. 220.

Christianity bears a huge burden of guilt." He advocates a return to pan-theistic values, where all creatures are seen as equals: "A democracy of all God's creatures."

This conflict points to the necessity for a clarification of the issue. Is Christianity the cause of the ecologic crisis? Does Christianity justify the wanton despoliation of the environment for the wants of man? Is Christianity being accurately represented here, or are these accusations properly directed towards a caricature of the dominion ethic? And what is the dominion ethic of Christianity?

Before directly addressing the questions posed above, a quick look at the historical development of environmentalism as a school of thought is in order. Its belief system has only recently become a coherent, viable force in the shaping of the public consciousness, but its roots date back to at least the Romanticist movement of the late 18th/early 19th centuries. Deism, the view which saw the universe as a vast clock- [203] like mech-anism set in motion by God, had failed to satisfy the emotional longing of the human soul, its need for intuitional, transcendental experience with the mystical or divine. The mechanistic, "billiard ball" universe which offered so much hope to the constructors of rationalistic philoso-phy had become a prison. Logic had excluded intuition and inspiration, yet their claims to the heart could not be so easily overridden by the for-mer's appeal to the head. Inevitably the backlash to secular sterility came, involving a flight to pantheistic experience of oneness with the Infinite. The mechanistic view of nature was replaced with an organismic one.

In young America, this trend received great impetus through the Tran-scendentalists, Emerson and Thoreau being their chief exponents; today they are patron saints of environmentalism. Emerson emphasized the or-ganic relationship of man to nature, of nature's being "the mirror of the soul." Oneness with God for him was the natural condition of every man open to nature's ethereal pulse, who could find fulfillment not in separa-tion from her but in harmony with her. Nature was the expression of God's essence, and man was her highest creation, nurtured in her bosom, delighting in her bounty. A process of mutual fulfillment in as-yet-unre-alized evolution was man's destiny with her.

The rise of Darwinism in the mid-19th century brought inevitable con-flict with this romanticized view of nature. Here the deistic mechanism which rationalism had previously proposed as the model of Creation gave way to that of a chance-determined process of natural selection. Darwin applied the Malthusian interpretation of the course of life to nature, nailing it firmly down with the concept (succinctly described in the title) *The Origin of Species by Means of Natural Selection or the Preservation of Favoured Races in the Struggle for Life.* There was some correlation between the two views in that both involved a concept of continuity of being and also turned away from the Christian God of *ex nihilo* creation. Yet Darwin's hypothesis involved quite a strained view of Mother Nature; Transcendentalism's emphasis on her beneficence and benignity were hard to reconcile with Darwinism's "red in tooth and claw" paradigm of nature. The enthronement of the ultimacy of chance by Darwinism also brought about unsolvable dilemmas for those with a romantic view of nature.

Notwithstanding such intellectual difficulties, environmental concern as a separate school of thought got underway with the publication in 1863 of George Perkins Marsh's *Man and Nature,* a ground-breaking [204] work which called attention to the deterioration of the environment on account of man's cultural advance. Marsh was an orthodox Christian who grounded his position in the Biblical teaching of righteous stewardship of the natural heritage: "Man has too long forgotten that the earth was given to him for usufruct alone, not for consumption, still less for profligate waste."[105] This emphasis set the tone for future development of conservation philosophy; (contrary to environmentalist dogma espoused today, it can be seriously doubted if effective environmental concern would have been produced, had Scriptural teaching not made up such a large part of the intellectual inheritance of the time).[106]

---

[105] George Perkins Marsh, *Man and Nature* [David Lowenthal, ed.] (Cambridge, Mass.: The Belknap Press of Harvard Univ. Press, 1965), p. 36.

[106] "All over the globe and at all times... men have pillaged nature and disturbed the ecological equilibrium ... nor did they have a real choice of alternatives. If men are more destructive now ... it is because they have at their command more powerful means of destruction, not because they have been influenced by the Bible. In fact, the Judeo-Christian peoples were probably the first to develop on a large scale a pervasive concern for land management and an ethic of nature."

Subsequent development also benefited, however, from the notions of state-oriented progress which came into vogue after the Civil War. Already in Marsh, one notes hostility towards private enterprise, and the call for increasing governmental control and regulation of natural resources. Environmental degradation was increasingly seen as wholly the production of unfettered special business interests.[107] Bureaucracy came to be seen as the salvation of the natural heritage: statist control, administered by professional, scientifically trained experts. "Wise use," "the greatest good for the greatest number in the long run" came to be watchwords. Then came the rise of the Progressive Republicans, who stood against the conservative, *laissez faire* wing of the party. Theodore Roosevelt was their chief leader; Gifford Pinchot was the ideological exponent of the conservation movement it nurtured.

Pinchot was the first native American trained in forestry. Under his leadership the U.S. Forest Service was established, and through the influence he had with Roosevelt vast amounts of Western acreage were set aside as federal reserves. Pinchot did not advocate setting them aside as preserves, but managing them for "the public good." This policy was designed to mollify Westerners dependent upon the timber and grasslands for their economic well-being, while protecting the lands from the rapacious special interests. It ran into trouble, however, not so much with these, but with another constituency of the conservation movement—the preservationists.

John Muir was a leader of the opposition to utilization of state-owned

---

René Dubos, *A God Within* (New York: Charles Scribner's Sons, 1972), p. 161; quoted in Tucker, *op. cit.*

[107] However, Tucker writes that "one of the greatest confusions about both the Conservation Movement and current-day environmentalism has been the idea that they pit 'the public' against 'the special interests,' or 'big business.' This is not the case. Since the beginnings of our history, the major environmental and conservation battles have pitted the land- and growth-hungry masses against a smaller minority that was attempting to husband resources under the principles of aristocratic stewardship. If anything, 'big business' has usually been a spectator to these conflicts. And ... big business has often been on *the side* of the conservationists and opposed to unrestricted development." Tucker, *op. cit.*, p. 47.

natural resources. He carried on the Transcendentalist tradition in that
wilderness for him was a spiritual haven:

> Muir infused his prose with the religious echoes he detected in his wil-
> derness temples: "The grand priest-like pines held their arms above us in
> blessing." Again: "Meadows grassed and lilied head-high, spangled river
> [205] reaches, and currentless pools, cascades countless and untamable in
> form and whiteness, groves that heaven all the valley!"[108]

But, as Graham points out, "Muir's reverence for the forest was pagan
rather than Christian."[109] In keeping with this "sacred grove" tradition,
Muir campaigned for the preservation of wilderness from any pressure for
utilization by man.

Pinchot and Muir were destined to be antagonists; preservationists
and conservationists split over the issue of use vs. non-use. This conflict
became apparent in what has come to be seen as a landmark in the history
of environmentalism, the Hetch Hetchy Valley confrontation. Hetch
Hetchy was a beautiful river valley located less than twenty miles from
Yosemite. Another of its "neighbors," however, was the city of San Fran-
cisco, which wished to convert the valley into a reservoir.

> This remote mountain valley, which Muir called a "wonderfully exact
> counterpart of the great Yosemite, not only in its crystal river and sub-
> lime rocks and waterfalls, but in the gardens, groves, and meadows of its
> flowery, park-like floor," also had certain characteristics that appealed to
> the city's engineers. The water carried through the valley by its "crystal
> river" was sweet and pure. Its "flowery, park-like floor" was flat, suggesting
> an ideal bottom for a reservoir. And its "sublime rocks" formed steep
> cliffs narrowing at one end into a slit that would be convenient and rela-
> tively cheap to dam. The floor of the valley was about three and a half
> miles long and it lay 150 miles from San Francisco.[110]

[108] Frank Graham, Jr., *Man's Dominion* (New York: M. Evans and Co., Inc,
1971), p. 151–2.
[109] *Ibid.,* p. 152.
[110] *Ibid.,* p. 160.

Pinchot led the charge for converting the valley into a reservoir; Muir anchored the resistance. For upwards of 13 years the battle raged, but in 1913 Congress passed a bill allowing construction of the dam to proceed. It was a victory for the advocates of "wise use," yet it would be seen as the Alamo of the yet-to-be-formed environmentalist movement.

The philosophy which Pinchot and the "progressive conservationists" espoused became the reigning dogma of statist land-use management. Government agencies have since proliferated in this century, especially with the impetus of the New Deal. Their adherence to "wise use" management philosophy kindled the opposition movement which was incipient in the preservationists of Muir's time. With the end of World War II came a huge increase in the number of people interested in public lands not for purposes of utilization, but for recreation. Increasingly as well came the disillusionment with material progress which [206] spawned a Romanticistic return to the organic view of nature. Aldo Leopold's *Sand County Almanac* preached ecological awareness and nature's intrinsic rights. Rachel Carson's *Silent Spring* warned of the dangers of the use of pesticides upon the fabric of life. These developments spurred the formation of the modern environmentalist movement, totally adverse to technological exploitation of nature, and dedicated to changing the management philosophy of the government bureaucracies from "wise use" to one of biocentric, harmonious interrelationship.

As has been noted, the notion of man's oneness with nature is the reigning presupposition of environmentalism. Thus environmentalism is often spoken of as being *biocentric,* that is, as making nature as a whole the focal point of value. Man is not above nature, but a part of her; as such he is considered of equal value with other animals and plants. The ecosystem as a whole is considered as a unit: its stability and integrity are made of uppermost importance. Right and wrong are then judged in terms of this standard. Aldo Leopold stated it this way: "A thing is right when it tends to preserve the integrity, stability, and beauty of the biotic community. It is wrong when it tends otherwise."[111]

Biocentricity is reinforced by Darwinian theory, which is another pillar of environmentalist thought. Man and nature are products of an evo-

---

[111] Leopold, *op. cit,* p. 240.

lutionary process of the struggle for life against a hostile, impersonal environment. There is no Savior-God ordaining that which comes to pass; chance is the backdrop against which life has come into being.

The necessary implication of this view of life is statism, as Gary North has shown.[112] The socialistic impulse is pervasive among environmentalists, because salvation is seen to lie in the hands of a planning elite. If society is to be ordered biocentrically, it must be done through this centralization of power, for the vast majority of people care more about themselves than they do about other species of life. Yet they are of no more value than these other species; so in order to properly integrate the ecosystem, planning by ecologically enlightened leaders is necessary. Human survival is seen as at stake in the maintenance of the integrity of the ecosystem, which integrity can only be preserved through centralized planning. The capitalist system is perpetrator of ecological destruction, and must be replaced. Barry Commoner typifies the sentiment here:

> [Commoner's] analysis points to the eventual necessity of a planned, rational, socialist economy because capitalism is inherently wasteful in its irrational pursuit of profit maximization instead of a rational and efficient use of energy, labor, and capital.[113]

These values lie behind environmentalist public policy agendas. Putting land into public (that is, state) ownership and then making sure that agency policy is biocentric are the measures of success. The text used as an introduction to wildlife biology on the university level makes this clear:

> The principal goal for any government wildlife agency, state or federal, is to *maintain viable populations of the wild species of America,* living so far as is possible, in their natural habitats. If that goal is accomplished, the

---

[112] Gary North, "From Cosmic Purposelessness to Humanistic Sovereignty," Appendix A in *The Dominion Covenant: Genesis* (Tyler, Texas: Institute for Christian Economics, 1982).

[113] Joseph M. Petulla, *American Environmentalism: Values, Tactics, Priorities* (College Station: Texas A&M Univ. Press, 1980), p. 70.

agency can be given credit for having done its job well.[114]

Most lands are in private ownership, and commonly the owner does not give wildlife conservation a high priority among the purposes for which he or she uses and manages the land.[115]

[P]ublic lands amount to over 760 million acres in the United States, with the greatest area in Alaska and the western states. According to Gustav Swanson: "Without these lands, the future of wildlife in the United States would be very grim for the onslaught of Homo sapiens is expected to continue."[116]

[T]hose to whom wildlife is important must play an active political role. Those wishing to exploit land for their own private benefit never cease their political efforts. Those who would protect the natural world cannot afford to do less.[117]

The anti-private ownership bias is evident. Salvation for the ecosystem is obtained by the work of collective man, who must organize and regulate society for the preservation of the ecosystem as a whole.

The biocentric orientation of environmentalism is its Achilles' heel. It is idolatrous to make the ecosystem the focal point of value. Psalm 24 states that "The earth is the LORD's, and the fulness thereof; the world, and they that dwell therein."[118] Valuation must come in terms of His Word.

Herbert Schlossberg succinctly states the issue:

Idolatry in its larger meaning is properly understood as any substitution of what is created for the creator. People may worship nature, money, mankind, power, history, or social and political systems instead of the

---

[114] Raymond F. Dasmann, *Wildlife Biology* (2nd ed.] (New York: John Wiley & Sons, 1981), p. 181.

[115] *Ibid.*, p. 184.

[116] *Ibid.*, p. 189.

[117] *Ibid.*, p. 191.

[118] [Scripture references in the appendix are from the King James Version.]

God who created them all.[119]

The ramifications of this idolatry include a decisive distortion of the [208] issue and a consequently perverted plan of action. In the case of environmentalism, the idol of material progress has given way to that of nature redivinized.

> Now that nature is no longer to be exploited, it is ready to be worshiped. It is still the whole show and we are still part of it, but now being part of it means that we no longer recognize anything that transcends it. For this mentality, the closer we are to nature and the further from civilization, the better off we are. The extreme hatred for human beings and corresponding love for animals that fills the satires of Jonathan Swift is coming into vogue ... Pure nature, hateful mankind.[120]

With this pantheistic view of nature, human beings lose their value as made in the image of God. There is no way to decide upon what portion of the ecosystem, and how much of it, is to be expended on human needs. All human action modifies ecosystems to some extent; the system which sees ecological integrity and stability as primary would then necessarily see satisfaction of human wants as subordinate to whatever measure of stability the ecologists happen to settle on. Yet Jesus said that we are of more value than many sparrows (Matthew 10: 31). Francis Schaeffer notes that "The economic dilemma of India is complicated by their pantheistic system, in which the rats and cows are allowed to eat up food that man needs. Instead of man's being raised, in reality he is lowered ... Man becomes no more than the grass."[121] The pantheistic, mystical view of nature is thus a primary cause of the poverty in many areas of the world.[122]

In addition to the ruin pantheistic values would bring to society, the

---

[119] Herbert Schlossberg, *Idols for Destruction* (Nashville: Th. Nelson Publishers, 1983), p. 6.

[120] *Ibid.,* p. 170.

[121] Francis Schaeffer, *Pollution and the Death of Man* (Wheaton, IL: Tyndale House Publishers, 1970), p. 33.

[122] P.T. Bauer, *Dissent on Development: Studies and Debates in Development Economics* (Cambridge: Harvard Univ. Press, 1976).

triumph of statism would bring about the repudiation, not the establishment, of environmentalist values. Bureaucrats are oriented towards acquisition and maintenance of power, which power is derived much more readily through the utilitarian exploitation of nature than its conservation.

> The more powerful the State, the more concentrated the control of economic resources available to State administrators, the more opportunities for economic control through monopolistic economic manipulation, the more ruthless will be those who satisfy their quest for power. The bigger the stakes, the more likely the least moral, most unscrupulous people will claw their way to the top.[123]

Unless the Stalins of this world harbor a soft spot for unspoiled wilderness, there can be little doubt that eco-values would be short-changed [209] under a socialistic regime. Even in a "free" society, bureaucracies tend to maximize agency benefits, whether or not they serve the public interest. Predation on the Treasury "commons" becomes an end in itself, rather than the common good being the end.[124]

The upshot of biocentricity is fittingly summarized by Schlossberg:

> The heaving sea of naturalism therefore casts up onto the shore two odd fish. One is he of whom Charles Reich is the exemplar: noumenal man, with a dreamy irresponsibility repudiating the rationality that makes possible what he values as well as what he hates, glorifying sensual experiences, and exalting attitudes and values that, widespread enough, would make it impossible for society to persist. Here is an antinomian egoism that by some miracle is expected to result in love and justice. The other is he heralded by the Galbraiths and the Skinners: phenomenal man, exalting rationality with a philosophy that makes reason impossible, submerging man into a nature that binds him irretrievably, giving him the status

---

[123] North, *op. cit.,* p. 97.

[124] John Baden and Richard L. Stroup, eds., *Bureaucracy vs. Environment: The Environmental Costs of Bureaucratic Governance* (Ann Arbor: The Univ. of Michigan Press, 1981); John Baden, ed., *Earth Day Reconsidered* (Washington, D.C.: The Heritage Foundation, 1980).

of brute or machine and, finally, taking charge in the name of survival. The phenomenal man is the one who kills Reich as a parasite who reduces the chance of survival. We have had prophets warning us about both specimens since early in the century, and we do not yet know which is the greater danger or which will gain ascendancy.[125]

Environmentalist values thus provide no way of providing for either the needs of man or those of nature. Environmentalism tries to safeguard nature's integrity by subordinating man to like creaturely status with the animal and plant kingdom. It tries to promote man's survival by making him aware of ecological interrelationships. Nowhere does it justify or regulate the exploitation of nature for the needs of man, provide for human rights, or resist the slide into totalitarianism. Its idolatry condemns it to outlandish and ineffective programs for the stewardship of the natural heritage, and subjugation to political expediency. May the Church be prepared with its own program for the righteous stewardship of God's creation, derived from His Word.

As has been noted, environmentalism is essentially a reaction to technology and material progress. It is spiritual heir of the Transcendentalist movement, embodying values consistent with a sacralized view of nature, and the necessity of organic harmony with her. As such it is a form of idolatry, in that it replaces the Christian view of creation and dominion with pantheism and escape from responsible stewardship before God. If nature is to be properly conserved, a framework consistent with God's Word is needed to guide the body of Christ in [210] stewarding the creation, which avoids the pitfalls of unrestrained exploitation on the one hand, and inability to provide for human need on the other.

That man is called to dominion over nature is made explicit in God's initial commandment to him (Genesis 1: 26–28). He, as made in the image of God, is above nature, and he is called to fill the earth and subdue it. The implications of this command are decisive.

In the first place, it is clear that nature was created for the benefit of man. From it he was to derive his sustenance (Gen. 1: 29). He was to cul-

---

[125] Schlossberg, *op. cit,* p. 173-74.

tivate it (Gen. 2: 15).[126] The animals were created as helpmeets for him (Gen. 2: 18–20). The biocentric perspective contradicts this, because man is placed on a par with the rest of creation.

Additionally, this dominion over nature was to be pursued familistically. God created man male and female (Gen. 1: 27), and created Eve as helpmeet for Adam in their common mandate. Rushdoony notes that

> Although originally only Adam was created (Gen. 2: 7), the creation mandate is plainly spoken to man in the married estate, and with the creation of woman in mind. Thus, essential to the function of the family under God, and to the role of the man as the head of the household, is *the call to subdue the earth and exercise dominion over it.*[127]

The family is thus the primary institution of dominion.

Ownership of the land is unavoidably an aspect of dominion. Psalm 24 affirms God's primary ownership, yet He delegates such to men.

> The earth is indeed the Lord's, as is all dominion, but God has chosen to give dominion over the earth to man; subject to His law-word, and property is a central aspect of that dominion. The absolute and transcendental title to property is the Lord's; the present and historical title to property is man's.[128]

Environmentalists characteristically advocate placing the ownership in the hands of the state ("public" ownership). Yet as the Bible calls man to dominion in terms of the institution of the family, it speaks of familistic ownership of property. "The scripture ... places property in the hands of the family, not the state. It gives property to man as an aspect of his dominion, as a part of his godly subduing of the earth."[129] *The stewardship of resources should be supervised by the most intensely committed social unit,*

---

[126] [At the time of writing I was still beholden to the received interpretation of this text. See references to Gen. 2: 15 in the Scripture index.]

[127] R. J. Rushdoony, *The Institutes of Biblical Law* [Vol. I] (Phillipsburg, N.J.: The Presbyterian and Reformed Publishing Co., 1984 [1973]), p. 163.

[128] *Ibid.,* p. 451.

[129] *Ibid.*

the family. It is not the only legitimate institution of ownership, but it is unquestionably the most universally recognized ownership [211] institution historically, and it is the social unit to which God originally announced the dominion covenant."[130] Thus the family is called to steward the creation in terms of private ownership.

To all of this must be added a time perspective. Dominion must be attained through a trans-generational orientation, that is, in terms of inheritance. Parents are to pass on to children the teachings and the tools that enable them to continue the extension of their dominion in the earth. Gary North calls this *familistic capital:* "Capital is to be used faithfully, expanded, and directed into the hands of one who will continue the faithful administration of the assets. Capital is primarily familistic capital."[131] Economic growth is then a function of the extension of families in the land over time. In this light the command to population growth (Gen. 1: 28) must be seen.

Here again, environmentalism is at odds with biblical teaching. Population growth is seen as inimical to the preservation of the natural heritage. North gives a concise and absolute rebuttal to this perspective, which deserves quotation in full:

> Unquestionably, nothing can grow at a constant rate of increase forever. The effect of "positive feedback," meaning compound growth, is to push life against the inescapable limits of the environment. If, for example, the population of the world in the 1970's, some 4 billion people, were to increase at 1 per cent per annum for a thousand years, the world's population in human beings alone—not to mention the supplies of beef or other animals to feed them—would be over 83 *trillion.* Either the rate of increase slows eventually to zero, or less, or else we run out of time. But this is precisely the point: *exponential growth, meaning compound growth, points to a final judgment, the end of time.* If the growth process is God-ordained in response to a society's covenantal faithfulness, then the day of judgment should become the focus of men's concern and hope. His-

---

[130] Gary North, *The Sinai Strategy* (Tyler, Texas: Institute for Christian Economics, 1986), p. 167.

[131] North, *op. cit,* p. 162.

tory is not unbounded. The zero-growth advocates assume that resources are finite, that history is indefinite, and therefore growth has to be called to a halt eventually. The Christian response is different: *growth is legitimate and possible, resources are indeed limited, and therefore the end of history will arrive before the growth process is reversed,* assuming society does not first return to its ethically rebellious ways, thereby bringing on temporal judgment (Deut. 8: 19–20; 28: 15–68). Any attempt to challenge the ethical legitimacy and economic possibility of an epoch of long-term compound growth that is the product of God's external blessings for covenantal faithfulness is nothing less than paganism. Such an attack is based on a philosophy of history which is unquestionably pagan, either cyclical time or [212] unbounded temporal extension. The goal of both views of history is the same: to deny the possibility of an impending final judgment. Compound growth points to final judgment, so humanists are faced with a major problem: either the growth must stop or history must end, and most Western humanists in positions of academic, economic, or political responsibility are afraid or unwilling to admit the existence of this dilemma. They want endless progress and growth, and the "numbers"—compound growth rates matched against finite resources—testify to the impossibility of achieving both goals. A few have become zero-growth advocates; most simply prefer to ignore the problem.[132]

These are the basic aspects of the dominion mandate. This mandate must be prosecuted covenantally, however, and not in autonomy of God. This is the key difference between secular and Scriptural dominion. Secular dominion operates in terms of human needs, wants, or desires. Scriptural dominion operates in terms of God's commandments.

It has been noted that environmentalism is a response to technological progress. This "progressivism" was, in turn, a secularized form of the dominion mandate—it is a *parody* of that mandate. Pollution, degradation, and despoliation of the environment are effects of man's rebellion, of Adam's fall. Since then, man has operated in terms of what *he* has wanted to do, not what God has wanted him to do. The result of this with respect to the environment has been an alternating wanton exploitation of it, or

---

[132] *Ibid.,* p. 175.

an abject subjugation to it. Yet the dominion mandate partakes of neither of these; its prosecution, conducted covenantally before God, results in both the dominion of man and the fulfillment of nature.

This can be understood when we see that the fall of man has resulted in the creation's subjection to "vanity" (Romans 8: 20) and "bondage to corruption" (v. 21). Paul says that "we know that the whole creation groaneth and travaileth in pain together until now" (v. 22). Man's sinfulness redounds to the corruption of nature. Such passages as Isaiah 24: 4–6 chronicle this result: "The earth mourneth and fadeth away, the world languisheth and fadeth away, the haughty people of earth do languish. The earth also is defiled under the inhabitants thereof; because they have transgressed the laws, changed the ordinance, broken the everlasting covenant. Therefore hath the curse devoured the earth, and they that dwell therein are desolate: therefore the inhabitants of the earth are burned, and few men left."[133]

Yet Paul speaks as well of the redemption of the creation from this [213] condition: "For the earnest expectation of the creature waiteth for the manifestation of the sons of God ... Because the creature itself also shall be delivered from the bondage of corruption into the glorious liberty of the children of God" (Romans 8: 19, 21). He thus ties this redemption intimately with the rule of the righteous. The covenant of grace, then, encompasses the dominion mandate, as in Christ the curse is lifted. The pride, selfishness, and greed of humanity are replaced with meekness and humility. And this, far from resulting in an escape from dominion, is its restoration.

Jesus Christ described Himself as "meek and lowly in heart" (Matt. 11: 29, rendered "gentle and humble" by both Moffatt and BV). He described Himself as such in relationship to those who sought Him. In His relationship to the Pharisees and Sadducees, Christ's conduct was firm and resolute. As Christ used the term meekness, it meant *not* the surrender of dominion, but rather the wise, merciful, and gracious use of do-

---

[133] [As is clear from the treatment of these texts in this book, my position has shifted away from this interpretation. See references to these verses in the Scripture index.]

minion. We *cannot* understand the meaning of meekness in Scripture unless we realize that it is not the surrender of dominion but rather the humble and godly use of dominion that it has reference to. The blessed meek are the tamed of God, those harnessed to His law-word and calling, who shall inherit the earth (Matt. 5: 6). The blessed meek are those who submit to God's dominion, have therefore dominion over themselves, and are capable of exercising dominion over the earth. They therefore inherit the earth.[134]

The covenantal use of the natural heritage then involves not only cultivation, but also conservation (Gen. 2: 15).[135] This is the twofold character of righteous stewardship. The Mosaic law provided for soil conservation and also wildlife conservation in the Sabbath ordinances. Rushdoony notes that the Sabbath symbolized the rest and release of redemption and regeneration for all of creation, and that "(the great work of restoration, of undoing the work of the Fall, includes the soil also. By this rest, the soil also is restored and revitalized."[136] In Leviticus (25: 7) it is stated that, among others, "for the beast that are in thy land, shall all the increase thereof be meat" during the Sabbath rest for the land. The first ordinance for the protection of wildlife in man's history was a part of the Mosaic law, specifically Deuteronomy 22: 6.[137]

Such examples make clear that a place is to be left for nature in the kingdom of God. It must be understood, however, that nature is subordinate to man, to be utilized in the first place for his benefit. Man in submission to God is to fill the earth and subdue it. Christ is Lord of heaven and earth since His ascension to the right hand of the Father, [214] who has put Him "far above all principality, and power, and might, and dominion, and every name that is named, not only in this world, but also in that which is to come: and hath put all things under his feet" (Eph. 1: 21–22). His kingdom is extended through His chosen: "and [the Father]

---

[134] Rushdoony, *op. cit,* p. 450.

[135] [See n. 126 above.]

[136] *Ibid.,* pp. 142–3.

[137] Class notes from a wildlife biology course given in spring 1982 by Prof. James D. Fraser, Va. Polytechnic Institute and State Univ.

gave him to be the head over all things to the church, which is his body, the fulness of him that filleth all in all" (vv. 22–3). Thus through the church the kingdom is extended, to the extent that the church is established. The fulfillment of the kingdom is seen in such prophecies as Isaiah 11: 6–9 and 65: 25, where the wild kingdom is tamed, and brought into the fellowship of the kingdom. This is the fulfillment of the Father's eternal purpose: "That in the dispensation of the fulness of times he might gather together in one all things in Christ, both which are in heaven, and which are on earth; even in him" (Eph. 1: 10).

This is the fulfillment of the dominion mandate, and this is what makes it essential. We cannot escape this calling, nor seek to prosecute it apart from God. We must work to complete this task; as Jesus said, "Occupy until I come" (Luke 19: 13). Renunciation is as sinful as wanton exploitation. Our task now is to bring, in the various fields of natural resources management, "into captivity every thought to the obedience of Christ" (2 Cor. 10: 5); that is, into conformity with the categories of thought revealed in Scripture.

BIBLIOGRAPHY

Alexander, T. Desmond. *From Eden to the New Jerusalem: An Introduction to Biblical Theology*. Grand Rapids, MI: Kregel Academic, 2008. ebook.

Alvarado, Ruben. *A Common Law: The Law of Nations and Western Civilization*. 2nd ed. Aalten, the Netherlands: WordBridge Publishing, 2019.

—. *A Theology of Nature*. Aalten, The Netherlands: WordBridge Publishing, 2020.

—. *Calvin and the Whigs: A Study in Historical Political Theology*. Aalten, the Netherlands: Pantocrator Press, 2017.

—. *The Debate that Changed the West: Grotius versus Althusius*. Aalten, the Netherlands: Pantocrator Press, 2018.

—. *Trojan Horse: Natural Rights and America's Founding*. Aalten, NL: WordBridge Publishing, 2022.

Beale, G. K. *The Temple and the Church's Mission: A Biblical Theology of the Dwelling Place of God*. Downers Grove, IL: InterVarsity Press, 2004.

Beisner, Calvin. *Where Garden Meets Wilderness: Evangelical Entry into the Environmental Debate*. Grand Rapids, MI: Acton Institute for the Study of Religious Liberty/Wm. B. Eerdmans Publishing Company, 1997.

Bellomo, Manlio. *The Common Legal Past of Europe, 1000–1800*. Trans. Lydia G. Cochrane. Washington, D.C.: The Catholic University of America Press, 1995.

Berman, Harold. *Law and Revolution: The Formation of the Western Legal Tradition*. Cambridge, MA: Harvard University Press, 1983.

Block, Daniel I. "To Serve and to Keep." *Keeping God's Earth: The Global Environment in Biblical Perspective*. Ed. Noah J. Toly and Daniel I. Block. Downers Grove, IL: IVP Academic, 2010. 116–140.

Botkin, Daniel. *25 Myths That Are Destroying the Environment: What Many Environmentalists Believe and Why They Are Wrong*. Guilford, Connecticut: Taylor Trade Publishing, 2017.

—. *Discordant Harmonies: A New Ecology for the Twenty-First Century*. New

York: Oxford University Press, 1990.

Breier, Idan. "Animals in Biblical and Ancient Near Eastern Law: Tort and Ethical Laws." *Journal of Animal Ethics* 8.2 (2018): 166–181.

Carson, Rachel. *Silent Spring*. Boston: Houghton Mifflin Company, 1962.

Chilton, David. *Paradise Restored: A Biblical Theology of Dominion*. Tyler TX: Dominion Press, 1985.

Commoner, Barry. *Science and Survival*. New York: Viking Press, 1966 [1963].

—. *The Closing Circle: Nature, Man, and Technology*. New York: Alfred A. Knopf, 1971.

Duby, Georges. *The Knight, the Lady and the Priest: The Making of Modern Marriage in Medieval France*. New York: Pantheon, 1983.

—. *The Three Orders: Feudal Society Imagined*. Chicago: University of Chicago Press, 1980.

Dumbrell, William J. *Covenant and Creation: An Old Testament Covenant Theology*. 2nd. Milton Keynes: Paternoster, 2013.

—. *The End of the Beginning: Revelation 21–22 and the Old Testament*. Homebush West NSW, Australia: Lancer Books, 1985.

Dyrness, William A. *Let the Earth Rejoice!: A Biblical Theology of Holistic Mission*. Westchester, IL: Crossway Books, 1983.

Ellicott, Charles John, ed. *An Old Testament Commentary for English Readers by Various Writers*. London: Cassell, Petter, Galpin & Co., 1882.

Granberg-Michaelson, Wesley. *Ecology and Life: Accepting Our Environmental Responsibility*. Waco, TX: Word Books, 1988.

Hall, Douglas John. *The Steward: A Biblical Symbol Come of Age*. Grand Rapids, MI: Wm. B. Eerdmans Publishing Company, 1990.

Hayek, Friedrich. *Law, Legislation and Liberty*. 3 vols. Chicago: University of Chicago Press, 1973-1979.

Hyneman, Jared and Christopher Shore. *Why Are We Stewards of Creation? World Vision's Biblical Understanding of How We Relate to Creation*. Natural Environment and Climate Issues, 2013.

Kantorowicz, Ernst. *The King's Two Bodies: A Study in Medieval Political Theology*. Princeton: Princeton University Press, 1957.

Kline, Meredith G. *Kingdom Prologue: Genesis Foundations for a Covenantal Worldview*. Overland Park, KS: Two Age Press, 2000.

Leopold, Aldo. *A Sand County Almanac.* Oxford: Oxford University Press, 1949.

Lieber, Francis. *On Civil Liberty and Self-Government.* 3rd. Philadelphia: J. B. Lippincott & Co., 1874.

Mauro, Philip. *The Number of Man: The Climax of Civilization.* New York et al.: Fleming H. Revell Company, 1909.

Mauser, Ulrich W. *Christ in the Wilderness: The Wilderness Theme in the Second Gospel and its Basis in the Biblical Tradition.* Naperville, IL: Alec R. Allenson, Inc., 1963.

McIlwain, Charles Howard. *Constitutionalism: Ancient and Modern.* Ithaca, NY: Cornell University Press, 1947.

Morales, L. Michael. *Who Shall Ascend the Mountain of the Lord? A Biblical Theology of the Book of Leviticus.* Downers Grove, IL: InterVarsity Press, 2015.

Niebuhr, H. Richard. *The Purpose of the Church and Its Ministry: Reflections on the Aims of Theological Education.* New York: Harper & Row, Publishers, 1956.

Noordmans, Oepke. *Liturgy in the Reformed Tradition.* Aalten: Pantocrator Press, 2018.

Och, Bernard. "Creation and Redemption: Towards a Theology of Creation." *Judaism* 44.2 (1995): 226–243.

Radbruch, Gustav. *Rechtsphilosophie.* 8th. Stuttgart: K.F. Koehler Verlag, 1973.

—. "Von Individualistischen zum sozialen Recht." *Der Mensch im Recht.* Göttingen: Vandenhoeck & Ruprecht, 1957.

Reich, Charles. *The Greening of America.* New York: Random House, 1970.

Reumann, John. *Stewardship and the Economy of God.* Grand Rapids, MI: William B. Eerdmans Publishing Company, 1992.

Skinner, Quentin. *Foundations of Modern Political Thought.* 2 vols. Cambridge: Cambridge University Press, 1978.

Southern, R. W. *Western Society and the Church in the Middle Ages.* London: Penguin Books, 1970.

Stark, Rodney. *The Victory of Reason: How Christianity Led to Freedom, Capitalism, and Western Success.* New York: Random House, 2005.

Strayer, Joseph R. *On the Medieval Origins of the Modern State.* Princeton, NJ:

Princeton University Press, 1970.

Tolkien, J.R.R. *The Letters of J. R. R. Tolkien*. Ed. Hunter Carpenter and Christopher Tolkien. Boston: Houghton Mifflin Company, 1981.

Ullmann, Walter. *A History of Political Thought: The Middle Ages*. Harmondsworth, Middlesex, England: Penguin Books, 1965.

Van Dyke, Fred, et al. *Redeeming Creation: The Biblical Basis for Environmental Stewardship*. Downer's Grove, IL: InterVarsity Press, 1996.

Walton, John. *The Lost World of Adam and Eve: Genesis 2–3 and the Human Origins Debate*. Downers Grove, IL: InterVarsity Press, 2015.

Wenham, Gordon. "Sanctuary Symbolism in the Garden of Eden Story." *Proceedings of the Ninth World Congress of Jewish Studies: Division A: The Period of the Bible*. Ed. David Assaf. Jerusalem: World Union of Jewish Studies, 1985. 19–25.

Westermann, Claus. *Genesis 1–11: A Commentary*. Trans. John J. Scullion. Minneapolis, MN: Augsburg Publishing House, 1984 [1974].

White, Lynn. "The Historic Roots of Our Ecologic Crisis." *Science* 155 (1967): 1203–1207.

Wilkinson, Loren, ed. *Earthkeeping in the Nineties: Stewardship of Creation*. Grand Rapids, MI: Wm. B. Eerdmans Publishing Co., 1991.

—. *Earthkeeping: Christian Stewardship of Natural Resources*. Grand Rapids, MI: William B. Eerdmans Publishing Company, 1980.

Young, Richard A. *Healing the Earth: A Theocentric Perspective on Environmental Problems and their Solutions*. Nashville: Broadman & Holman, 1994.

INDEX OF SCRIPTURE REFERENCES

GENERAL INDEX

CPSIA information can be obtained
at www.ICGtesting.com
Printed in the USA
JSHW011117070623
42856JS00005B/9

9 789076 660714